COME
AND
SEE

Born of the Spirit
English Canadian Catechetical Series
CCCB

Contents

Welcome . . .

. . . to your new program, **Come and See.** A large group of fine and dedicated teachers and writers has worked very hard to present you with a delightful book. Boys and girls like yourselves from all across Canada have also helped to make the program special for you.

The work they prepared holds many surprises, and all of them are meant to deepen your understanding and friendship with the Lord Jesus.

I know they enjoyed preparing this book for you and I hope that you will have as much enjoyment in using it. May you be enriched with your love of the Lord Jesus and may you want with all your hearts to serve him.

Yours sincerely,

Marcel Gervais,
Bishop of Sault Ste. Marie

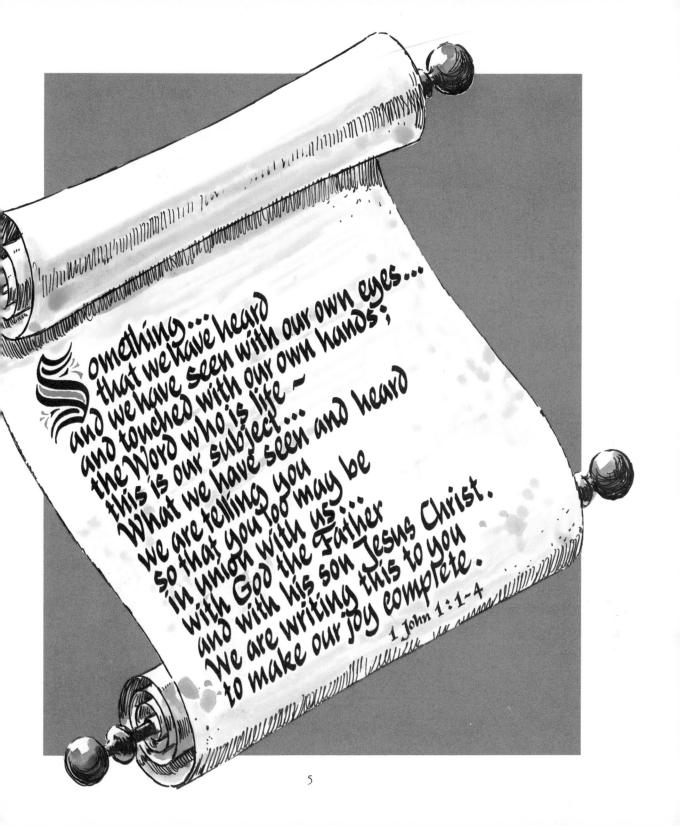

Something...
that we have heard
and we have seen with our own eyes...
and touched with our own hands;
the Word who is life –
this is our subject...
What we have seen and heard
we are telling you
so that you too may be
in union with us...
with God the Father
and with his son Jesus Christ.
We are writing this to you
to make our joy complete.

1 John 1:1-4

New beginnings

Gathering

How do we gather?

Where do we gather?

Why do we gather?

Hi, my name is Philip. Here are the secrets of my code!

What's your class story?

Breadmaking

The magic hour had come. Everyone was there and the house was filled with excitement. Aunts, uncles, and cousins — they had all come to celebrate the day. Laughter echoed in the dining room as the family gathered around the huge oak table for the special morning meal. Suddenly, the kitchen door burst open and the hot golden bread was carried high to Mario's place at the head of the table. The room blushed with hugs and handshakes and kisses, then fell to a hush as all eyes turned to the young boy who had made this special day come true.

"We're a family!" he said as he took one of the golden loaves. He felt a joy inside him that was like a river flowing out of a dry land. He wanted to sing and dance and twirl about for the sheer energy inside him. Then for a moment he just wanted to hold the bread and remember how they had made it. Together.

Not so long ago, they had gone shopping among walls of green cucumbers and soft red tomatoes. She taught him all the little things, like how to shop, how to buy food and bring it home. And she had taught him to call her Nonna because that was the way they said Grandma in the Old Country. He was Mario. She was Nonna. And they were best friends. Nonna was big on the Old Country. In the evening, when the sun hung low and orange in the sky, Mario liked to perch on Nonna's fluffy feather bed to hear stories of long, long ago. Mario thought that Nonna was the best storyteller in the whole world, and he rested his head on the soft hump of her knees. This was their dream-time together, when grandfathers and great-grandparents came alive and joked and laughed and did wonderful things.

Everyday they were together, Mario and Nonna. They laughed when things were light and happy. They cried when things were heavy and sad. But their favourite time, more than all the other times, was their baking time, when they got together in the warm, cozy kitchen to make Easter bread. That was special, and Nonna taught him all the things he needed to know.

"Be careful you don't crack the eggs, Mario," she said. "If they crack they're no good to put in the little nest of Easter bread. Our pane di pasqua — that's what we call it in Italian." And the brightly coloured eggs glistened in the water, waiting to take their place of honour on the top of the soft bread.

"Do you make it just for Easter?" Mario asked. "No, for special breakfasts too. We could make it for your First Communion. I remember we had it in the Old Country, when your father was baptized, and when your grandfather and I were coming to this country." Then Nonna started to talk about that other time, when Mario's grandfather and father and

Nonna had first come here, and how lonely and strange they had felt in the new land. But they had stayed together, and worked and learned and laughed. "We were a family then, Mario!"

Mario thought a long time about their coming to this country. It was as if the new land had made them a promise, and so they had stayed.

On Good Friday, Mario made his promise to Nonna. They were baking bread together. He watched as her strong fingers pressed deep into the dough. When she became tired, he slipped in to take her place. "You remind me of your father when he was your age," she said. "He used to help me too, you know. But then he got big, went away and forgot about our family customs. No time to help his mother in the kitchen." Mario knew that she was sad about that.

"Don't *you* forget, Mario," she said.

He looked up. "I won't Nonna. I promise."

You could tell that he meant forever. The promise was like gold.

(Adapted from *Grandma's Bread.*)

THINK ABOUT IT . . .

What was the *promise?*
How did Mario and Nonna keep it?
How was it like gold?

The story of Pentecost

When Pentecost day came round, Peter, John, James, Andrew and the rest of the twelve were together in one room. Several women disciples were there also, including Mary, the mother of Jesus. Since Jesus had died, they often gathered together to pray. They felt alone and afraid. They felt lost, like sheep without a shepherd.

This is what Scripture tells us:

"They had all met in one room, when suddenly they heard what sounded like a powerful wind from heaven, the noise of which filled the entire house in which they were sitting; and something appeared to them that seemed like tongues of fire; these separated and came to rest on the head of each of them. They were all filled with the Holy Spirit" (Acts 2: 1-4).

Since Pentecost was a Jewish harvest festival, people had come to Jerusalem from every nation in the world known at that time. At the sound of this great and powerful wind, all these people gathered together.

Then a marvellous and wonderful thing happened.

FINISH IT . . .

Can you finish the story? Share your story endings with the class!

MAKE YOUR OWN . . .

Plan a kite-making day! Decorate your kites with Pentecost words, signs and pictures.

Remember

Pentecost is the day when the Spirit of Jesus helped the disciples spread the good news. We celebrate the birthday of the Church on Pentecost Sunday.

Unit 1

The Church hands on the story of Jesus

Tradition:
where are we coming from?

What traditions are being handed
on in these photographs?

Why do you think people want
to preserve their traditions?

What do our traditions tell
us about who we are

- as a family?
- as a people?
- as a community?
- as a country?
- as Church?

WRITE IT DOWN . .

Sometimes, when
people are finishing
great buildings, they
make a collection of things
and seal them into a wall as
a "time capsule." That way,
people of the future will
know more about the history
of the building and the
people who made it. If you
were making a time capsule
for your family, what would
you collect? What about a
time capsule for your
community?

An Ancient Time Capsule!

CHECK IT OUT . . .

Who did the scrolls belong to?

Why were they hidden in the caves?

What did Muhammad do with the scrolls?

Why do you think these scrolls are such great treasures?

Do you know what we call them?

◄ *"Jars from Qumran in which some of Dead Sea Scrolls were found."*

These goats of mine! One of them has wandered off again. What a handful these creatures are! My father tells me, "Muhammad, look after the goats. You are old enough to take this responsibility!" But such a responsibility! — Roza, come back! Where are you, Roza?

What's this? I never saw this hole here before. How could I have missed it? But it's just an old hole in the ground.

What's that? A stone — I must have kicked it — it has bounced into the hole and landed far, far down inside. And something is broken down there. I heard it crack! I'm getting out of here!

This was the beginning of an historic adventure for a boy and his friends. A day or so later, Muhammad returned with his cousin to explore the hole he had stumbled on earlier. The hole was the entrance to a cave, where the boys found some leather scrolls rolled up in linens and stored in jars. The scrolls turned out to be precious writings from long ago. Muhammad's curiosity led him to a great discovery.

Summer, 1947

"Elizabeth, receive from the Church the Good News of Jesus Christ . . .

May it touch your mind, your lips and your heart."

"We thank you, God."

Something... that we have heard and we have seen with our own eyes... and touched with our own hands; the Word who is life ~ this is our subject... What we have seen and heard we are telling you so that you too may be in union with us; with God the Father and with his son Jesus Christ. We are writing this to you to make our joy complete.

1 John 1:1-4

The parish family is part of a larger family, the Church. For hundreds of years the Church has treasured and handed on the stories of Jesus — what he said, what he did, what others said and wrote about him. We are a people with a great story.

The Church hands on to us Jesus' story in the New Testament, sometimes called the Gospel Book.

One day a friend of Jesus wrote a letter to some Christians which tells us why this book is so special.
◄ This is what he wrote.

THINK ABOUT IT . . .

Why is it so important for John to share what he has seen and heard?

tradition:

the handing on from generation to generation of customs, beliefs and practices.

Remember

From its very beginning the Church has handed on the good news of Jesus Christ.

We explore the book of the good news

The **Bible** is the most precious of all our books. We sometimes call it the "Book of the Word of God." Like Jesus, the Bible is God's "I love you" to the world.

Although the Bible is just one book, it is much like a library of books!

It is divided into two parts: the Old Testament and the New Testament. The Old Testament tells the story of God's love before Jesus was born. The New Testament continues God's love story. It is about the life of Jesus and his message of the kingdom.

The New Testament is made up of 27 books!

Use the New Testament collection to help you find all 27 books. Decide where to fit them in the columns.

Gospels	Acts of the Apostles	21 Letters	Revelation
The story of the good news of Jesus according to: ■ Matthew ■ Mark ■ Luke ■ John	Luke's story of the friends of Jesus after his death and resurrection	Letters written by followers of Jesus to different people and Churches	A book written to give hope to Christians that Jesus will give life even when things are very hard

There are different translations of the Bible. Look at your New Testaments. What version do you have? Good News? Jerusalem Bible? Revised Standard Version?

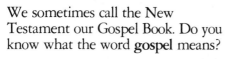

We sometimes call the New Testament our Gospel Book. Do you know what the word **gospel** means?

This year we will explore the good news and discover more about the story of Jesus using the four Gospel accounts of Matthew, Mark, Luke and John. Matthew, Mark, Luke and John are called **evangelists**.

Finding Your Way Around the Bible

Each book of the Bible is divided into chapters. A chapter is divided into verses. A verse is usually one or two sentences. Verses are marked with smaller numbers. The name of the book is always at the top of each page.

If you look closely at the picture on this page you will see that it is the story of your good friend, Zacchaeus. Now, pick up your own New Testament and find Luke 19: 1 and the story of Zacchaeus for yourself!

When we see **Luke 19: 1-10**, we read it this way: "The Gospel according to Luke, chapter 19, verses 1 to 10."

How would you read the following?

Matthew 13: 31-32; John 14: 1;
Mark 10: 13-14.

To Catholics of the Byzantine-Ukrainian Church, the Gospel Book is precious.

Here are some of the ways that the Byzantine-Ukrainian community shows reverence for God's word:

The Gospel Book is beautifully decorated.

It is always kept on the altar.

The priest kisses the Gospel Book when he first comes to the altar.

Short acclamations are sung before the word is read.

The book is incensed to show reverence to Christ, present in his word.

TAKE A MOMENT . . .

Look at the Gospel Book covers. What do you see? What does it mean?

How do Catholics of the Roman Church show reverence for the Book of God's Word?

N E W   W O R D S

Bible:
comes from the Greek words **ta biblia** which means "the books."

gospel:
comes from an old English word **god-spel** which means "good news."

evangelist:
a messenger of good news of victory.

Remember

The four Gospels of Matthew, Mark, Luke and John tell us the *good news* of Jesus Christ.

The story gets started

From memory to manuscript

It was discovered early this morning that the sacred writings belonging to the Christian community have all disappeared. Nowhere can any Bibles be found! The Christian community is in a state of panic! Alarm is spreading everywhere!

How can we help preserve the story of Jesus?

How can we prevent the story from being lost?

■ Recall your favourite story or quotation from your Gospel Book and write it down.

■ Get together with the rest of the class and make a class manuscript out of your work.

Long ago when Bibles were copied by hand, monks gave their whole lives to **manuscript writing**. They worked long and hard to make the Bible pages as beautiful as possible, decorating them with great care and illuminating them with gold leaf.

"I have said these things to you
while still with you;
but the Advocate, the Holy Spirit,
whom the Father will send in my name,
will teach you everything
and remind you of all I have said to you."

John 14: 25-26

Do you remember this New Testament passage?

When did Jesus make this promise to his disciples?

Follow the monks' example and carefully decorate your Bible passage.

Can you imagine how the Gospels were composed back in the first century?

What would people want to remember and celebrate about Jesus?

How do you think the word of God spread?

How the Gospels Came to Be

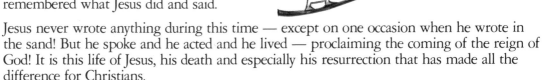

1. Jesus of Nazareth
His life, death and
resurrection 27-30 A.D.

At the heart of the Gospels
was the memory of the person
of Jesus. His friends
remembered what Jesus did and said.

Jesus never wrote anything during this time — except on one occasion when he wrote in the sand! But he spoke and he acted and he lived — proclaiming the coming of the reign of God! It is this life of Jesus, his death and especially his resurrection that has made all the difference for Christians.

2. The Christian Communities
after the resurrection 30-65 A.D.

Having met the Lord after his
resurrection, the apostles and other
disciples *preached* or *proclaimed*
that Jesus is risen. They baptized those who believed the good news and *celebrated* the risen Lord in the eucharist.

Those who listened to the word and believed that Jesus was the *Christ*, the *Messiah* were called *Christians*. These Christian communities called themselves *Church* which means "gathering."

Little communities of Christians or churches started first in Jerusalem and other parts of Jesus' country, Palestine. Then, as the apostles began to travel to neighbouring countries, other churches grew up.

Everywhere they went, the apostles spread the good news about Jesus' resurrection. They handed on the story of Jesus by word of mouth. That is why we call it the teaching of the apostles or the **apostolic tradition.**

During this time, the disciples of Jesus *remembered his words and deeds*, choosing their stories to suit the needs and understanding of the communities who listened to them. Soon people began to learn the stories by heart, repeating them over and over again in their communities.

3. Putting the stories of Jesus together 65-100 A.D.

During this time, people collected and sorted out the accounts of what Jesus said and did. Each of the four evangelists . . . Mark, Matthew, Luke and John . . . selected from the stories and sayings of Jesus and arranged them into stories for their communities.

Remembering Jesus' promise, "I will send you the Spirit who will lead you to complete truth," the evangelists recorded the words and actions of Jesus that they proclaimed in the early Christian communities. (See John 16: 13.)

We take paper for granted — we see large amounts of it every day.

But in biblical times, writing materials were much harder to come by. That is because it took a long time to make such materials.

A reed called *papyrus* was cut to show its inner stem. These inside parts were cut into strips and laid out on a hard surface, some lengthwise and some crosswise. Then, the paper-maker would crush the stems, hitting them with a mallet until they stuck together, forming a sheet. When the sheet was dry, it was rolled up into a scroll.

Storing a number of scrolls was a problem, because they took up so much room. By about the second century, people discovered that they could flatten sheets of papyrus and hold them together to form a *codex*, and our present-day book came to be.

The earliest complete manuscript of the New Testament is the Codex Sinaiticus. This manuscript is written in Greek on parchment. It dates from the fourth century A.D. ▼

DID YOU KNOW?

Apostolic tradition:

the teaching of the apostles by word of mouth about the risen Jesus.

Remember

There are three stages in the formation of the Gospels:

the life, death and resurrection of Jesus

the life of the Christian communities

putting the stories of Jesus together.

The first followers encounter Jesus

A t Bethany, on the far side of the Jordan River, John the Baptist was baptizing. As he stood there with two of his disciples, Jesus passed by. Staring hard at Jesus, John pointed to him and said, "Look, there is the Lamb of God."

Hearing this, the two disciples — Andrew and John by name — followed Jesus. Jesus turned around, saw them following and asked, "What do you want?" They answered, "**Rabbi**"— which means Teacher — "where do you live?"

"Come and see," he replied; so they went and saw where Jesus lived and stayed with him the rest of the day only. (See John 1: 35-39.)

CHECK IT OUT...

Was the "Come and see" invitation for one day?

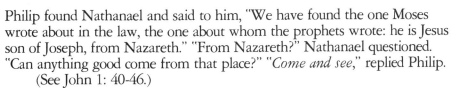

Early the next morning Andrew had exciting news for his brother, Simon. "We have found the **Messiah**" — which means the Christ — Andrew exclaimed, and he took Simon to Jesus. Jesus looked hard at Simon and said, "You are Simon son of John; you are to be called **Cephas**" — meaning Rock.

The next day, after Jesus had decided to leave for Galilee, he met Philip and said to him, *"Follow me."* Philip came from the same town, Bethsaida, as Andrew and Peter.

Philip found Nathanael and said to him, "We have found the one Moses wrote about in the law, the one about whom the prophets wrote: he is Jesus son of Joseph, from Nazareth." "From Nazareth?" Nathanael questioned. "Can anything good come from that place?" *"Come and see,"* replied Philip.
(See John 1: 40-46.)

Turn the page and find Bethsaida, Galilee, Nazareth and the Jordan River on the map.

What do you think Philip meant when he said, "Come and see"?

Later on, as Jesus was walking throughout Galilee, he met a man named Matthew sitting by the customs house. Jesus said to him, *"Follow me."* Matthew got up and followed Jesus.
(See Matthew 9: 9.)

Do you think it was exciting meeting Jesus? What did Matthew do? Andrew? Philip?

MAKE YOUR OWN . . .

Choose your favourite fabric and design a *Come and see* banner for your classroom!

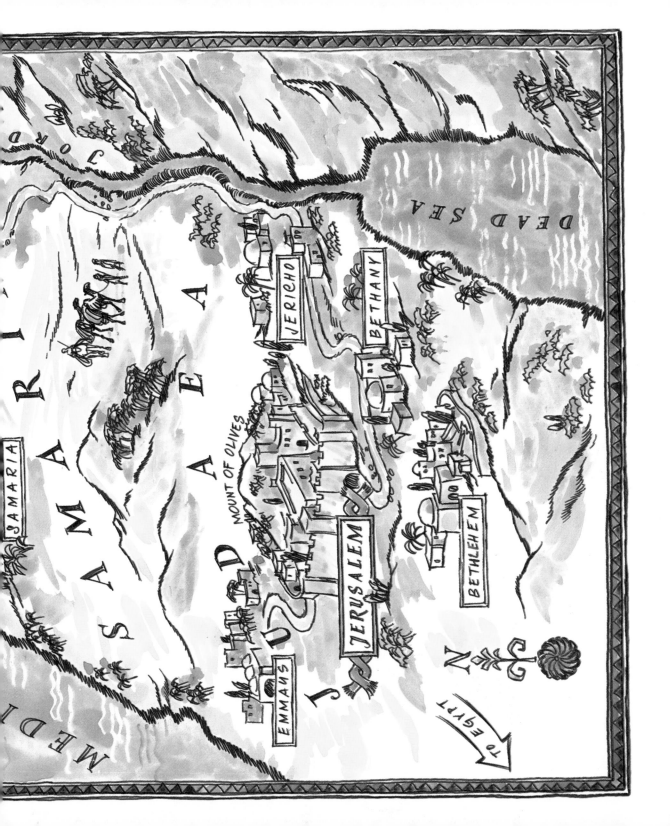

Come and See

It was just another crisp September morning for Maurice. Just another school day — all except for one thing. Today he and his Grade 4 class were going to reveal the secrets of their pendant codes! Maurice's limp was eager as he made his way to St. Anthony's Elementary in the brisk morning air.

The Grade 4 class had worked hard all week preparing their pendants; making the dough, designing their secret codes, painting them on. They pulled ribbons through tiny holes in the hard dough, so they could hang their pendants around their necks. Now the time had come!

The children gathered in a small cozy circle on the classroom floor. Everything soon grew quiet, except for the glow of the large Christ candle that flickered fast shadows against the classroom wall.

The teacher handed a skein of yarn to the first storyteller who began to share the secrets of her code. As she told her story to the class, she rolled the yarn into a ball. The storyball grew bigger and bigger as one student, then another, took a turn. All of a sudden Maurice found himself holding the storyball and from the stillness in the room he could tell that the class was anxiously awaiting his story.

Holding the ball of wool steady in his hand, Maurice stared out at the little circle of people. Somehow he knew that the story he would share today would be the story of a lifetime. Gently he laid the ball in his lap and steadied it with his right paralyzed arm. Maurice reached for the pendant that hung round his neck.

"I have chosen an M for my code," he said. "M stands for Maurice, Mary and Mother. This past summer I was able to be with my mom and I was happy. M is special to me."

The number 10 was visible as Maurice slowly turned over his pendant. "Ten years ago, when I was born, I nearly died," Maurice continued. "Ten stands for ten years of life."

His classmates were feeling Maurice's story. "I have something else to say," Maurice blurted, as he let go of the pendant and reached for the storyball. "For a long time I have come to school with my handicap. For a long time I have felt left out and alone."

There was a long silent pause before Maurice spoke again and his dark eyes filled with tears.

"Today, as I roll my story, I don't feel left out anymore. For the first time I feel I belong, I belong here. It's the greatest feeling."

TAKE A MOMENT . . .

How do you think the class felt after Maurice's story? Do you think they finally understood why Maurice had been silent all those years?

Do you think they told others about what happened?

How is this story a "Come and See" story?

Think of ways that the Lord Jesus invites us to follow him today. Mime your thoughts for your friends.

N E W   W O R D S

rabbi:
means "teacher."

messiah:
means "Christ" or "the anointed one."

Cephas:
means "rock."

Remember

Philip's words to his friend Nathanael: "We have found the one Moses and the prophets wrote about. He is Jesus son of Joseph, from Nazareth."
(See John 1: 45.)

Crowds are attracted to Jesus

What is happening in these pictures?

Why do you think such huge crowds gather around these people?

A Gift of Joy

The boy tossed an orange into the air. Then another, a third and finally a fourth. He kept the four oranges moving from hand to hand, arching above his head.

People stopped to watch. They smiled and laughed with the boy in the patched clothes who juggled almost everything on the fruit vendor's stand — oranges, apples, lemons.

Giovanni was an orphan. He had neither parents nor a home. He juggled for food and the pleasure of making people smile and laugh. As Giovanni grew older, he became better and better at the one thing he could do well. For years he wandered from town to town, juggling for food and a place to sleep, wearing the face and clothes of a clown.

His most famous act was done with seven coloured balls. He began with a violet ball. Then he tossed up a blue ball. Green, yellow, orange and red balls followed. Faster and faster he juggled the balls so that they seemed to melt together. The arching, speeding balls looked like a rainbow.

People shouted to Giovanni to go faster and faster, higher and higher. At the peak of the action, he would add a gold ball to resemble the sun. People laughed and cheered.

Giovanni spent all his life juggling to make people smile. His rainbow act became famous all over Italy.

(Adapted from *A Gift of Joy* by Janaan Manterach)

Have you ever met people like Giovanni who drew crowds because of something they did well?

Great crowds gather around Jesus

Look these passages up in your New Testaments and finish reading about the events.

"The whole town came crowding around the door . . ." (Mark 1: 33).

"So many people collected that there was no room left, even in front of the door" (Mark 2: 2).

"People were bringing little children to him . . ." (Mark 10: 13ff).

"He now went up into the hills and summoned those he wanted. So they came to him . . ." (Mark 3: 13).

"Again he began to teach by the lakeside, but such a huge crowd gathered around him that he got into a boat on the lake and sat there" (Mark 4: 1).

For more crowd stories, read:

Mark 1: 35-38	Mark 1: 40-45
Mark 2: 13	Mark 3: 7-10
Mark 3: 31	Mark 6: 30-44

THINK ABOUT IT . . .

What is it about Jesus that makes people want to meet him?

Imagine

Jesus and his disciples are in Bethsaida. Jesus has just cured a blind man. You are there! Standing on the shore of the Sea of Galilee, you see the afternoon sun dance on the blue waters. The disciples of Jesus are standing around.

What's the general feeling on the lakeshore?
What are the friends of Jesus saying?

You begin to walk north with Jesus toward Caesarea Philippi. The disciples are talking with him. As you walk along, you hear Jesus ask a question: "Who do you say that I am?"

As you think of the right words with which to answer him, the disciples speak up.

"You are John the Baptist!"

"You are Elijah!"

"You are one of the prophets!"

Jesus then turns to Peter and says to him, "But you, who do you say that I am?" You look up at Peter. "You are the Christ," he replies in a clear voice.

Then Jesus looks your way.

Remember

Peter's response to Jesus: "You are the Christ."
Mark 8: 29

What do you say or do?

Jesus is a storyteller

Totem poles

Long ago the Amerindians of Canada's Northwest Coast spent long hours constructing totem poles to tell their stories. Their lives and their beliefs are documented on these poles!

Totem poles were made from tall cedar trees. Skilled artists carved the logs and painted them, using paints made from fish oil, berry root, charcoal and other natural ingredients.

Totems belonged to the Amerindian families who put them up. The carved figures on a family totem pole represented the names, rights and possessions of the family. The figures helped the family remember its stories and traditions. Totem pole figures were carved to look like humans, birds and animals. The animals often displayed human faces and hands, sitting or standing up straight like human beings.

It was a time of great celebration when a totem pole was ready to be raised and set upright in the village. People gathered to feast and to dance. They gathered especially to hear the family storyteller tell stories about the figures on the pole!

Today families are holding on to their tradition and carving new poles on Canada's Pacific Coast. They are coming together to feast, dance and share stories at the raising of the totem poles.

"Every symbol on the totem pole has a meaning," explains Mrs. Caroline Mickey. The symbols on this totem pole have been explained to us by the artist, Charlie Mickey. This carving tells the story of one of the West Coast's Chiefs and of his ten sons. At the top is the Thunderbird, and the mask on the breast of the Thunderbird represents the youngest son in the story following. Next, the sea serpent represents a source of help to the Thunderbird. Lower down, the grizzly bear is symbolic of the inner strength of the Indian people and their desire to achieve. Below, the whale is a symbol of the hunt and a source of food. And last, at the bottom, the owl is symbolic of the wisdom of the Native people.

This carving tells the story of one of the West Coast's Chiefs and of his ten sons.

Totem pole carving by Charlie Mickey of Hesquiat Tribe, Port Alberni

For many years the eldest nine sons of the chief had tried to harpoon a great whale which was their main source of food. They failed to kill the whale and always came home empty handed.

So one day the youngest son heard the thundering noise of the Thunderbird, which was the sign that there was a whale close by.

He had never been permitted to go out on the great whale hunts so he decided he would go out and catch the whale and bring it home.

He told his father he was going and the older brothers did not believe that he could bring this large whale in. Using the brothers' canoe, floats and ropes, he and a crew of five men set out to bring this large whale in to shore.

So when they came up on the great whale, he harpooned it but did not kill it, and the whale towed him right out to sea. They saw no land or mountains for many days as they were towed around. Finally, one day they came to an island which was barren and the whale went right up on the shore, taking the chief's youngest son and his crew along with him. For many days they sat around not knowing what to do, only hoping they would survive.

One day while the youngest son was sleeping he was awakened by a little bird which was going to show them their way back home. On this day the large whale turned around and towed them off the island and back to where he was first harpooned. The whale then died in the water and the youngest son of the chief towed the whale back to shore.

The youngest son's family, thinking him to be dead all those days, had discarded all of his belongings.

The happiness and joy of the parents and his people of seeing him again was cause for much joy and celebration. The chief's youngest son towed the whale to shore and the people all carried a section of the whale up the beach.

After this, the people thought of him as the greatest hunter of them all.

Carving of the Ksan pole at the Museum of Anthropology

CHECK IT OUT . . .

What figures would you carve on a totem pole?
What experiences and events would you document?
What stories would you want to remember?
Paint a sketch of your totem.

Jesus and parables

Jesus was a fantastic storyteller. He used parables to tell stories about God, about God's reign and about people. Jesus used parables like the Amerindians used totems to tell stories about life. Parables are to Jesus what totems are for the West Coast people.

Parables are like windows through which we see God at the heart of life; in yeast and mustard seeds, in pearls and wheat. Parables help us see with new eyes God's dream of a world filled with peace, justice and love.

Jesus was the storytellin' kind.
He painted pictures in the mind.
It was the way he showed people how
*   things were supposed to be.*
He used the sky. He used the sea.
He used the birds. He used the tree.
He used whatever he could see.
Storyteller?
Yes, Jesus was the storytellin' kind.
He painted pictures in the mind.
It was the way he helped us see
what we — you and I — could really be.

(From *Experiencing Jesus* by Mark Link)

The kingdom of heaven is like the spoonful of yeast that you spill into the bread mix. But what happens to the bread mix? (See Matthew 13: 33.)

The kingdom of heaven is like treasure hidden in a field. But what happens when someone finds the treasure? (See Matthew 13: 44-46.)

The kingdom of heaven is like a mustard seed. But what happens to a mustard seed when we plant it in the earth? (See Matthew 13: 31-32.)

Do you remember those parables? Look them up in your New Testaments and enjoy the images.

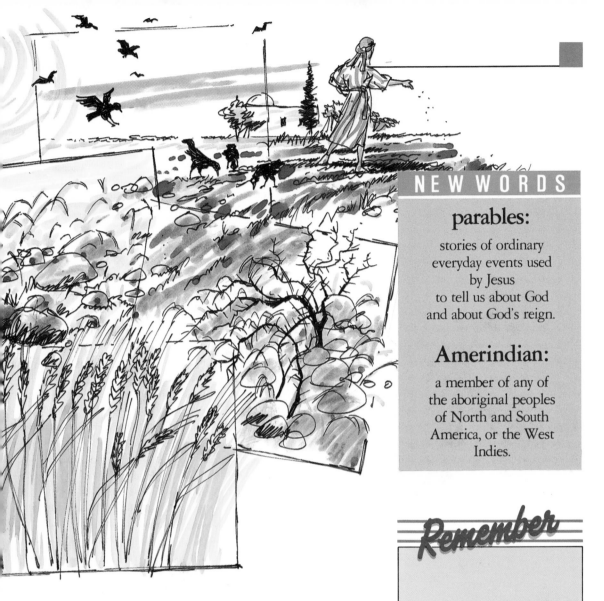

Remember

Parables help us
discover truths about
God, the kingdom
and ourselves.

The Sower

Every picture tells a story. Do you know the story that this picture tells? It is found in your New Testament.

Using the picture as a guide, write the story or tell it to a friend.

In parables Jesus tells us about the kingdom of God

Guess what's going on!

Open your remembering book and write down your guess.

Now, go to your New Testaments and read these parables:

Luke 15: 8-9
Luke 18: 10-13
Mark 4: 26-29.

Compare what you wrote with what you read.

A treasure hunt!

Do you have something that is precious to you? a letter? a photo? a book?

Take a look at the treasures on this page.
They come from all across Canada.

Labrador

This letter is my treasure. It was written to me by my grandmother. She was my best friend.

Prince Edward Island

This photo is my treasure. Cathy is with me at the seashore. She's my best friend. It's our first vacation together.

Ontario

Our piano is a treasure for me. I have played it for a long time and it has been in our family for many years.

Saskatchewan

These seeds are my treasure. They come from our first garden. I helped my family plant it last spring.

Seabottom Treasures

If you have ever seen or held a pearl, no doubt you understand why people think they are such treasures. They are smooth and cool and milky-white but with faint touches of colour too. People the world over agree: they are very beautiful.

Pearls form inside oysters which live at the bottom of the sea. If you could open an oyster shell, you would see that it is lined with a pearly sort of coating, called mother-of-pearl.

Sometimes, a grain of sand gets inside the living oyster's shell. This causes the little creature some discomfort, so it begins to cover the sand with a layer of pearly material called "nacre." It also rolls the sand around and around, trying to get it right out of the shell.

Over a long period of time, the nacre-covered sand becomes very round and hard — a pearl, in fact. The longer it is in the oyster's shell, the larger it grows and the rounder it becomes. Perhaps someday a very lucky person finds the oyster and opens it up, to find a valuable treasure. What a surprise!

In your opinion, what makes pearls so precious?

A Jesus parable

"Again, the kingdom of heaven is like a merchant looking for fine pearls; when he finds one of great value he goes and sells everything he owns and buys it" (Matthew 13: 45-46).

CHECK IT OUT...

In this parable, the merchant gives up everything he owns when he finds *the pearl of great price.*

In what way are the disciples like the merchant?

Did the disciples find a *pearl of great price?*

How did they know?

Elizabeth was excited, being in the great cathedral for the first time. There was so much to see that she could hardly pay attention to any one thing. But the stained glass windows at last held her interest. Deep reds and blues and greens seemed warm and friendly with the sun streaming through to make them bright.

Her mother, seeing Elizabeth's excited look, explained the story behind each pane of glass. She told Elizabeth that, in the days when people could not read books, they could understand the story of a saint's life by looking at the beautiful glass windows in the church.

The next day at school, Elizabeth's teacher wanted to know, "Does anyone know who a saint is?"

Elizabeth was ready with her answer. "A saint is someone the light shines through!"

Stained glass windows are a treasure in themselves. But they also tell stories about people who have found a great treasure — God's love for them. Back in the 1200s, a man named Richard lived in Chichester, England, and he too had discovered this treasure. He said this prayer every day to remind himself of the treasure he kept in his heart, like the merchant who kept a pearl in his pocket:

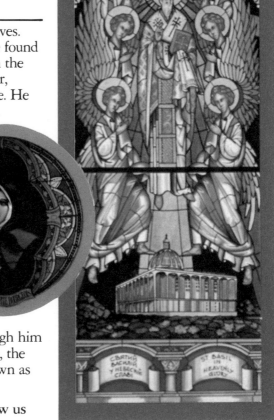

> Day by day,
> Dear Lord, of thee
> Three things I pray:
> To see thee more clearly,
> Love thee more dearly,
> Follow thee more nearly,
> Day by day.

The people who knew Richard saw how good and kind he was to everyone. The light of God's Spirit shone through him in love. This is why, not very long after he died, the Church proclaimed him a saint. He is now known as Saint Richard of Chichester.

Do you know persons today whose lives show us that they have found *the pearl of great price?*

Read this story about Mother Teresa of Calcutta and see the light of God's love shine through.

O nce in the streets of Calcutta I picked up a little girl. She was about six years old and I could tell from her face that she was hungry and hadn't eaten for days. I gave her a crust of bread and she started to eat it, slowly, one crumb at a time. I said to her, "Eat the bread, go on, eat it." And the child replied, "I am afraid, because when the bread is finished I shall be hungry all over again."

In our schools in Calcutta we give free bread and milk to all the children. I noticed one day that a little girl took her bread and hid it. I asked her why she was not eating the bread and she told me: "My mother is very sick at home. We have no food in the house at all and I want to take this bread for her to eat."

"That is real love, real sharing," said Mother Teresa. "Children could learn from that."

Once a little boy from a wealthy family in Calcutta was having a birthday. His parents always gave him a lot of presents and a big party. This year he asked them to give all the money they would spend on him to Mother Teresa. And on the morning of his birthday they brought him down in the car. He handed me an envelope with the money in it.

That child taught his parents so much. He taught them that sharing is love in action. Many children in Calcutta now do not invite their own friends to a birthday party. They come instead to our Children's Home and have the party there with our children as guests.

Mother Teresa smiled. "Tell children how important it is to share," she said. "Tell them that sharing is the most important thing in the world!"

(Mary Craig © Hamish Hamilton Ltd.)

THINK ABOUT IT . . .

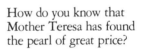

How do you know that Mother Teresa has found the pearl of great price?

Write her message on a banner and hang it in a special place.

Remember

The kingdom of heaven is like a merchant looking for fine pearls.

In parables Jesus tells us about God

Working as a shepherd

Sheep always know," says D'Alfonso, "that before they lie down for the night, their shepherd has figured out their grazing for tomorrow." Bedded down beside a pool of sparkling water under a clear starry sky, the sheep feel safe, knowing that their shepherd is with them.

Many of us have seen pictures of sheep with their shepherd, but few of us have actually met a shepherd guiding his flock. In Palestine where Jesus lived, a shepherd would have been with his sheep from the time he was a young boy. So he was close to them, just as you might be close to one of your pets.

Shepherds name their sheep and know each one by name. The sheep, in turn, know their shepherds, the sounds of their voices, the sounds of their flutes. Shepherds would do anything to protect their sheep, even die if they had to and sometimes that's just what happened in Palestine. A short time ago, a young shepherd was on his way from Tiberias to Tabor with his sheep, when the flock was attacked. Trying to defend his sheep, the shepherd died and was left on the roadside with his dead herd.

At every sheepfold you will find a big earthen bowl of olive oil and a large stone jar of water. As the sheep come in for the night, they are led to a gate. The shepherd stretches his rod across the top of the gateway just higher than the back of the sheep. As each sheep passes in single file, he examines it for injuries. If he finds one, he drops his rod across the sheep's back and the sheep steps out of line. The shepherd then carefully cleans the wound of his injured sheep. Dipping his hand into the olive oil, he anoints the injury. Following this, he brings a cup of cool water — never half full but always overflowing — to the sheep. Sinking its nose into the water clear to the eyes, the fevered sheep drinks.

When all the sheep are at rest, the shepherd lays his staff on the ground, wraps himself in his woolen robe and lies across the gateway facing his sheep. With his staff within reach, the shepherd closes his eyes for the night.

Wanted:

strong and healthy people to train as shepherds.

Requirements:

must like animals and the outdoors; enjoy being on the trail for long periods of time and be willing to lay down their lives for their sheep.

Apply in writing or come in person to:

Shepherds Inc.
R.R. # 1
Antigonish, Nova Scotia.

Jesus wanted to tell us how much God loves us. In a parable he said that God loves us the way a good shepherd loves his sheep. Here are some of its words:

Parable of the good shepherd

"I tell you most solemnly,
I am the gate of the sheepfold . . . .

Anyone who enters through me
*   will be safe:*
*   . . . will go freely in and out*
and be sure of finding pasture . . . .

I am the good shepherd;
I know my own
and my own know me,
just as the Father knows me
and I know the Father;
and I lay down my life for
*   my sheep."*
*   John 10: 7-15*

WRITE IT DOWN . . .

Look up John 10: 1-15 and read the parable.

Why do you think Jesus chose this parable to describe his message?

Make a list of all the reasons you think Jesus might have had for using it.

Share the list with your friends.

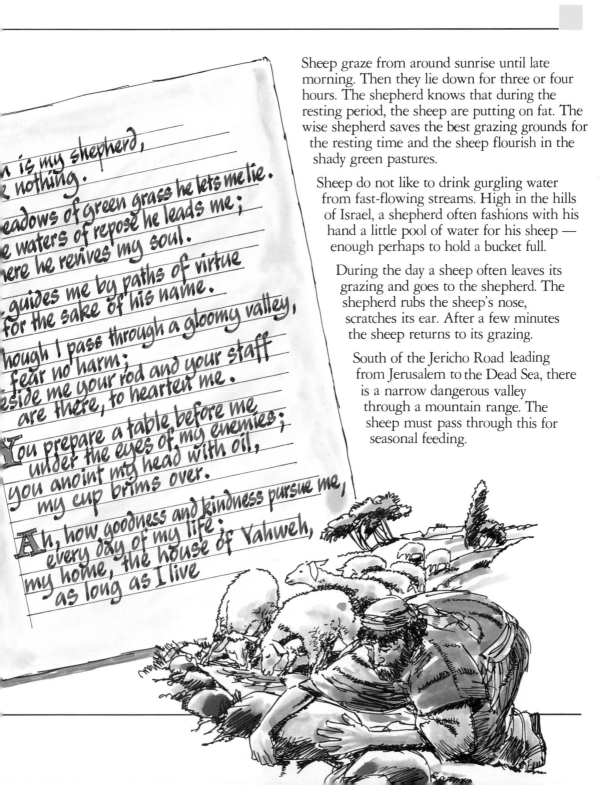

...n is my shepherd,
...e nothing.

...eadows of green grass he lets me lie.
...e waters of repose he leads me;
...here he revives my soul.

...guides me by paths of virtue
for the sake of his name.

...hough I pass through a gloomy valley,
...fear no harm;
...eside me your rod and your staff
...are there, to hearten me.

You prepare a table before me,
...under the eyes of my enemies;
you anoint my head with oil,
...my cup brims over.

Ah, how goodness and kindness pursue me,
...every day of my life:
my home, the house of Yahweh,
...as long as I live

Sheep graze from around sunrise until late morning. Then they lie down for three or four hours. The shepherd knows that during the resting period, the sheep are putting on fat. The wise shepherd saves the best grazing grounds for the resting time and the sheep flourish in the shady green pastures.

Sheep do not like to drink gurgling water from fast-flowing streams. High in the hills of Israel, a shepherd often fashions with his hand a little pool of water for his sheep — enough perhaps to hold a bucket full.

During the day a sheep often leaves its grazing and goes to the shepherd. The shepherd rubs the sheep's nose, scratches its ear. After a few minutes the sheep returns to its grazing.

South of the Jericho Road leading from Jerusalem to the Dead Sea, there is a narrow dangerous valley through a mountain range. The sheep must pass through this for seasonal feeding.

The valley is four and a half miles long. Its sidewalls are over 1500 feet high in places and it is only 10 or 12 feet wide at the bottom. Traveling through the valley is dangerous because its floor is cut with deep gullies. The sheep must jump across. The shepherd coaxes the sheep to take the leap and if they slip, he uses his staff. The old style crook is encircled around a large sheep's neck or a small sheep's chest, and the sheep is lifted to safety!

On the grazing grounds there are poisonous plants. Each spring the shepherd must be constantly alert. Going ahead of the flock, he carefully weeds out the poisonous roots.

In the evening, the injured sheep are cared for with olive oil and cool fresh water.

Safe inside the fold, the shepherd and the sheep lie down for the night.

Remember

"I am the good shepherd: the good shepherd is one who lays down his life for his sheep."
John 10: 14-15

A light shines in the darkness

"Bet you can't hit that tree!"

"Bet I can!" Tommy lets go of his toboggan and sets himself to fire at the smudgy oak. Whack! The snowball splatters. Then the two friends continue to trudge along in the deep crisp snow.

"I like winter," Aaron says. "I like snow and snowballs and snowpeople. I like tobogganing, too."

"I love tobogganing! It's my favourite!" Tommy is excited. "Hey, let's really go tobogganing! Let's try the big hill."

"You mean Ice Mountain?"

"Yeah! Let's make it the best afternoon ever," Tommy bubbles.

That's too far, Aaron thinks to himself. It's three o'clock already and the woods are thick. For a moment he is quiet. Then he catches the glow in his friend's eye and begins to feel the adventure. "OK. Let's do it!" They head off, toboggans trailing. On the far side of the valley, the trail is hard to see, but the sun is still strong. Time passes quickly as they run and slide up and down the steep slopes. Their laughter bounces over the hills, breaking the silence of the winter air.

Suddenly, Tommy thinks of home. "Hey, it's getting dark. Why so soon?" Aaron knows that it's past time to go. But they were having so much fun that evening has set in and they haven't even noticed. They haven't felt the snowflakes that are now falling fast.

"Remember at Hallowe'en, Tom, how long we had to wait until it got dark? Now there's more night than day. Isn't that strange?"

"Sort of scary," Tommy says. "Suppose every day it got darker and darker and one day the sun never came back."

"But it couldn't. We learned about that in science, remember?"

"I don't care what we learned. I want to go home."

As the boys walk on, they feel a soft wind on their backs. There are no stars in the sky. They enter the thick woods and pick their way through the tall trees. "The path must be over here some place," says Aaron, hoping to find an opening.

"I think we're lost!" Tommy wails.

The woods are darker now and the trees cast giant shadows. Without any light, every trace of a trail is gone.

"There's a storm blowing up," Aaron says. Their hearts beat fast as they hear sounds they have never heard before.

All at once, a huge wind shrieks through the woods. Icy pebbles begin to hit hard. The boys crouch under some low branches, shuddering. All they can do is wait in darkness.

When the wind seems to let up, Aaron is the first to speak. "We've got to get out of here and move on," he says, and they begin their way through the darkness once more.

Slowly, slowly a soft dim glow sets in between the shadows of the trees. "It must be the moon," they say. There, above a little clearing, is the most beautiful star-dotted sky the boys have ever seen. The moon streams down to light their way.

"We can do it now, Tom. I know the way." Aaron's voice is strong again. Quick as fireflies, the boys head for home.

MAKE YOUR OWN ...

Paint your favourite scene from the story.
Choose a line to go with it and create a shadow box.

When Father Herbert Dunlop of Vancouver, BC heard that you would be reflecting on light and darkness in this theme, he sat down and wrote you a message:

"In your story you have talked of light and darkness; the darkness that comes upon the world when the sun goes down; darkness that makes us afraid to be alone.

"But there is another kind of darkness. It has nothing to do with the sun going down in the evening . . . ."

What does Father Dunlop mean?

Christmas is coming the goose is getting fat. Time to put a penny in the old man's hat.

Time is running out! Christmas is just around the corner! Christians call this special waiting time Advent. It is getting-ready time, a time of hope. It is a time of *waiting in hope* for light! Sometimes, it's pretty hard to wait.

How are the people in these pictures making the light and hope of Advent come alive?

John the Baptist is a sign of hope

"Prepare a way for the Lord, make his paths straight."

For hundreds of years before the coming of Jesus, people were longing for the light, longing for signs of hope in the darkness of their lives.

"And then the word of God came to John, son of Zachariah and Elizabeth," Luke's Gospel tell us. John was living the life of a hermit in the wilderness of Judaea when this happened.

In the fifteenth year of the reign of Tiberias Caesar (about 27 A.D.), John knew in his heart that he was to be God's message of hope.

On the banks of the Jordan River, his message sounded forth:

Children of the Light

Refrain

We are children,
children of the light,
We are shining,
in the darkness of the night,
Hope for this world,
Joy through all the land,
Touch the heart of ev'ryone,
Take ev'rybody's hand.

1. *Come and gather round the flame,*
   share the light in his name,
   we are the children of the light.
   As the wind blows where it will,
   spread the news to ev'ryone,
   there's still plenty of time for
   we have just begun.

2. *Join the song of all the earth,*
   we've a dream, a dream to share,
   and a promise of rebirth.
   Let the earth feel the warmth of
   the love there in your heart,
   we have many a dream and promises
   to keep.

(© The Redemptorists — CSSR
Music, Toronto. Words and Music —
Eugene O'Reilly)

NEW WORD

Advent:
means "coming."

Remember

"Prepare a way for the Lord,
make his paths straight."
Luke 3: 4

John the Baptist bears witness to the light

He stood on the riverbank, shaggy and fierce in his appearance. And yet they listened.

The sun beat down, and no wind stirred to make the heat more bearable. And yet they listened.

Even the river, which usually splashed among the stones, seemed quiet while John the Baptizer preached. And they listened to every word he said:

"Repent, for the kingdom of heaven is close at hand" *(Matthew 3: 2).*

Meet Jenny and Joey

Jenny: What on earth happened to you?

Joey: What do you mean?

Jenny: Your hair . . . !

Joey: I'll have you know I paid a lot of money for this hairdo.

Jenny: I didn't mean to upset you, but your hair looked great just the way it was.

Joey: Thanks, but I *had* to change it.

Jenny: What makes you say that?

Joey: Don't you know what time of the year this is?

Jenny: Of course I do, it's December!

Joey: Besides that — What time of the church year is it?

Jenny: It's Advent, one of my favourite times because of all the special things we do to get ready for Christmas.

Joey: And Advent is a time for us to change. Don't you remember Father Don's homily last Sunday about John the Baptist? He said that John told people to prepare the way of the Lord by changing.

Jenny: So that's it! But John the Baptist didn't mean changing on the outside — things like your hair style or your clothes. He meant changing on the inside in the way that you love God and other people.

Joey: But how are people going to know that I've changed on the inside?

Jenny: They'll know by the good things that you do.

WRITE IT DOWN . . .

Write one way you can "change on the inside."

Make up an Advent puppet show and share it with your family and friends.

59

"Repent!"
Get ready for God!

The crowds who followed John the Baptist saw that he was very serious about what he had to say. His message was urgent because he was speaking for God.

John the Baptist was a great prophet who spoke out strongly in God's name. "Someone is coming," said John, "someone who is more powerful than I am, and I am not fit to undo the strap of his sandals" (Luke 3: 16).

John made people look at the darkness and sin in their lives. Longing in their hearts for the light that John promised, they asked him, "What must we do?" "Repent, for the kingdom of heaven is at hand," John said.

During Advent we also ask, "What must we do?" "How can we get ready to welcome the promised one, the true light?"

s
o
n
s
h
i
n
e

shine on   e   *eye shine*

shine out   I shine

I

A M

the

light   of
the world
light   of
the world
light   of
the world
light   of
the world
light   of
the world
light   of
the world
light   of
the world
light   of
the world
light   of
the world
light   of
the world
light   of
the world
light   of
the world

The Word was the true light
that enlightens all
peoples

Donna Kerrigan

Leader: *Let us prepare our hearts for the Lord by calling to mind our sins.*

Take a moment of silence and think back on your day.

Have I failed to love, to make someone happy? Have I failed to bring light where there was darkness?

Prayer: I confess to almighty God,
and to you, my brothers and sisters,
that I have sinned through my own fault.
in my thoughts and in my words,
in what I have done,
and in what I have failed to do;
and I ask blessed Mary, ever virgin,
all the angels and saints,
and you, my brothers and sisters,
to pray for me to the Lord our God.

NEW WORDS

prophet:
a person who speaks for God.

repent:
to "change our hearts" or "turn around."

Remember

" . . . Someone is coming, someone who is more powerful than I am . . ."
(Luke 3: 16).

Unit 4

We celebrate the light shining in the darkness

And we, with our unveiled faces reflecting like mirrors the brightness of the Lord, all grow brighter and brighter as we are turned into the image that we reflect; this is the work of the Lord who is Spirit (2 Corinthians 3: 18).

What do we do when we are in the dark?

We look for the light!

Lord Jesus, you are the Light of the world. Come among us and into our hearts today so that we can reflect your light, your love and your goodness to everyone we meet.

Mary, Mary

Refrain:

*Mary, Mary, highly favoured of
the Lord!
Mary, Mary, bearer of the living
Word,
All you are proclaims God's
endless fame.
For your faithfulness we hail the
name of
Mary, Mary, highly favoured of
the Lord!*

1. *Blest are you who kept God's
word,
trusted in all that you heard,
kept a faith-filled open heart
to the promise of the Lord.
Mary, you're the first to say
Yes to God in every way.
Be it done to me O Lord,
according to your word.*

2. *Mary, you have shown to us
how to follow, how to trust.
Teach us in the loving way
you believe in your own Son.
Holy Spirit, come to us,
give us faithfulness and trust.
Help us live as Mary did,
giving praise unto the Lord!*

God is with us

In the Byzantine Ukrainian church the Christmas Eve service is celebrated with great rejoicing. When the priest sings out the proclamation, "God is with us," a feeling of exultation fills the church and people sing over and over again "God is with us . . . rejoice . . . God is with us!"

God is truly with us. God is with us, a child is born to us: a Light has shone on us, a Light for all nations. God is with us in Jesus, whose name is Emmanuel.

Leader: God is with us. Give ear all you nations and be humbled, for God is with us. Upon us who dwell in the land of the shadow of death a great light has shone.

All: God is with us. Give ear all you nations, and be humbled, for God is with us.

Leader: For a child is born to us, a Son is given to us.

All: God is with us. Give ear all you nations, and be humbled, for God is with us.

Leader: God's power is upon his shoulder and his peace shall have no end.

All: God is with us. Give ear all you nations, and be humbled, for God is with us.

Leader: And he shall be called the messenger of the great wisdom of God.

All: God is with us. Give ear all you nations, and be humbled, for God is with us.

Leader: Wonderful, Counselor, the Mighty God, the Master, the Prince of Peace, the Father of the age to come.

All: God is with us. Give ear all you nations, and be humbled, for God is with us.

(Adapted from the great compline of the Feast of the Nativity of Christ)

Joseph and Mary present Jesus in the Temple

Look at the scenes on this page.

What do they remind you of?

How do these actions help light up Christmas?

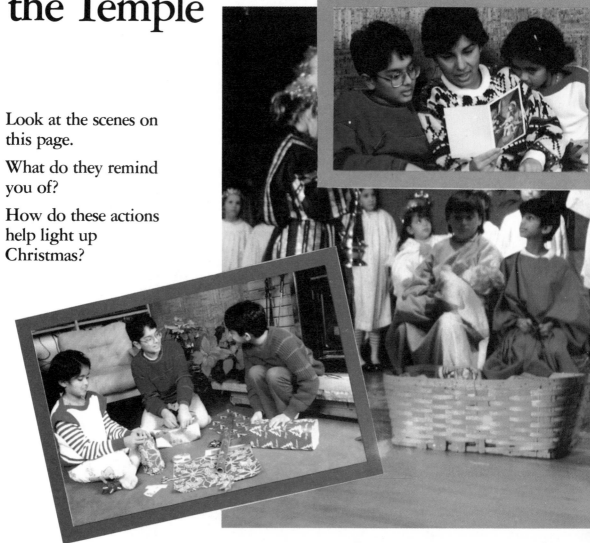

Who helped light up your Christmas?

Write a letter to thank that person for helping to light up your Christmas.

Let us pray.

Thank you, God, for showing us how to be lights for one another. Help us always to walk in your light, guided by your Holy Spirit.

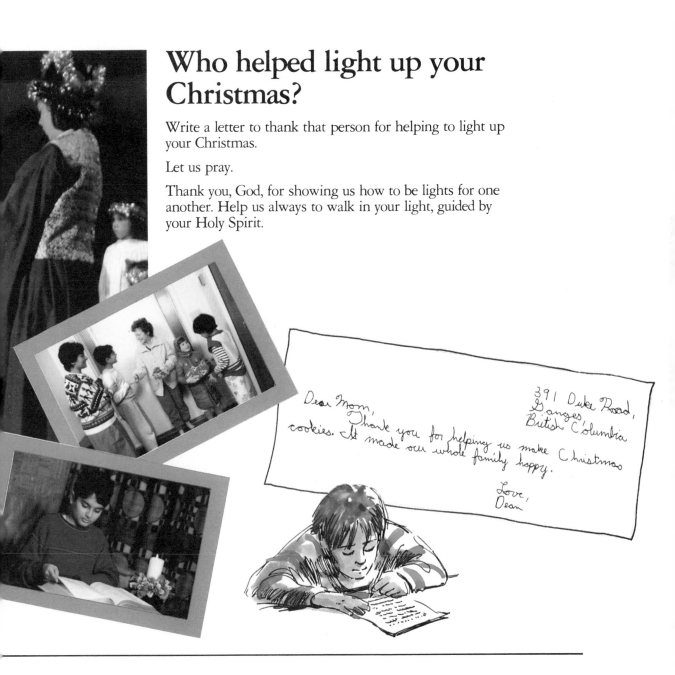

391 Duke Road,
Ganges,
British Columbia

Dear Mom,
Thank you for helping us make Christmas cookies. It made our whole family happy.

Love,
Dean

Joseph and Mary remember

"I remember," Mary said eagerly. "How could I forget! It was such a special day. We took Jesus to Jerusalem to present him to the Lord."

"I remember Simeon," Joseph's voice was clear. "It was just a wonderful scene. Simeon took Jesus in his arms and blessed God; and he said: 'My eyes have seen the salvation which you have prepared for all the nations to see.'"

J.H.
(News reporter):   Who did you meet when you entered the Temple?

Mary: Simeon and Anna.

J.H.:   Tell us what you remember about Simeon.

Mary: He was a very holy man who prayed special prayers for Jesus.

It seems Mary and Joseph were very impressed with Anna and Simeon. They kept saying Simeon's words all through the interview:

> "Thank you, God for keeping your promise. Now I am happy to die,
> for I have seen Jesus, the Light of the World!"

The Presentation song

When Simeon first saw
  Mary's child
His heart was filled with
  radiance bright;
He held him in his arms
  and sang
In praise of Jesus, child of
  light.

"Now I can die a happy
  man
My eyes have seen the
  wondrous sight
Of Jesus who will save
  the world,
The long awaited light of
  light."

Still Jesus shines upon our
  way,
And shows us how to live
  aright.
We hold our candles high
  and sing
In praise of Jesus, Lord of
  light.

Simeon and Anna
welcomed Jesus, the
Light of the world.

The National Gallery of Canada

Jesus' land and people

This is Israel — the homeland of Jesus. How long would it take to travel to Israel from where you are? by jet? by boat?

Use a roadmap to measure from your town to another town about 240 kilometers away. That's about the size of Israel!

Israel is special to many people. For Jewish people, it is a homeland. For Christians, it is special too. Each year thousands of people go to Israel to visit the places where Jesus lived and walked. Some of those journeys are called **pilgrimages**.

Do you know anyone who has taken a pilgrimage to Israel? What did they like best about their trip?

Pilgrims renew their baptismal vows in the Jordan River.

Let's go on a pilgrimage!

Beautiful Galilee was Jesus' home

Jesus was born in Bethlehem, but he spent almost all his life in the region of Galilee in the north. Unlike the south, Galilee at that time was very fertile, with rich farmland and lush green grasslands. Most Galileans were poor farmers who worked a small plot of land for a small share of the harvest. Jesus knew these people well and loved them.

Sea of Galilee

Here is the Sea of Galilee

This lake was probably called the "Sea" of Galilee (or Tiberias) because it was the only large body of water in the north. It is about 24 kilometres long and 11 kilometres wide. Jesus loved this lake.

Galilean countryside

Jerusalem is now in view

Jerusalem was the largest city in Palestine. It was built in the mountains overlooking the countryside below. Jerusalem had a great history, for the leaders of the Jewish people had lived here and defended it against invaders. It was in this city that one of their kings, a man named Solomon, had built the most beautiful temple to give honour to God.

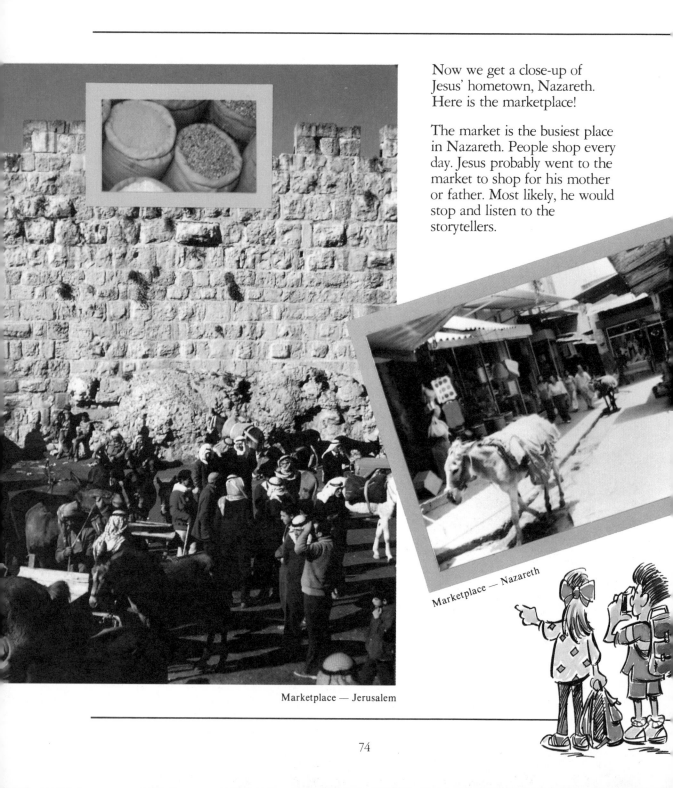

Now we get a close-up of Jesus' hometown, Nazareth. Here is the marketplace!

The market is the busiest place in Nazareth. People shop every day. Jesus probably went to the market to shop for his mother or father. Most likely, he would stop and listen to the storytellers.

Marketplace — Nazareth

Marketplace — Jerusalem

In Jesus' day the women came and went to the village well. Jesus probably helped Mary carry the large water jar and would also have enjoyed listening as people chatted with one another. There is still a well in Nazareth today, called "Mary's Well."▶

Workers in Jesus' time

One of the most important trades in Nazareth is the making of pottery. We can imagine that Jesus watched the village potter at work, shaping lumps of rich red clay on his wheel into bowls and water jars and oil lamps and then putting them to dry and harden in a kiln or oven.

Joseph was a carpenter so Jesus would know this trade well. With simple tools he would help Joseph make such things as tables, benches, stools, door frames, plows. Carpenters also made toys for children, such as dolls and spinning tops.

ng
l
th
of

and

At school

When Jesus was six years old he started going to school with other boys. School was held in the synagogue, often called the "House of the Book." There the boys would sit on a mat around their rabbi or teacher. Using as their textbook the Torah or the Scriptures, they learned to read and chant the psalms in Hebrew. Jesus spoke a language called Aramaic. Since they had no books there was a lot of memorizing and repeating of scripture verses. The boys practiced their writing by tracing the letters in the sand with a stick. They learned some simple mathematics and at the end of the day they would listen to the rabbi tell them wonderful stories about their people.

Jewish boy reads the Torah at his Bar Mitzuah

Playing games

Children in Jesus' day had to make up their own games. For example, they would dig a hole in the ground and see how many stones they could throw into the hole from a certain distance. They would also pretend they were adults, playing wedding and house and funeral. (See Matthew 11: 16-17.)

Nazareth

Here is a picture of Nazareth today. Jesus' house might have looked something like this.

The poorer people had one-room houses made of handmade, sun-dried bricks. The floors were mostly of earth, packed hard and worn smooth. The rooftop was flat, with a low wall around it and most often was reached by a ladder or outside stairway. Here the family spread grain and fruits to dry in the hot sun. When the weather was good, people did their chores on the roof. Every morning Mary probably ground grain for bread there on the rooftop. It was also a cool place to sleep.

In Jesus' day, the houses had very simple furnishings — the one room was both a living room and kitchen. Mats for sleeping were rolled up during the day. Every home had a pottery lamp which burned olive oil, and even in the poorest home this was kept burning all night.

What was it like?

If you don't mind,
if you've got the time,
could I ask you a few things
about when you were young?

Did you run here and there,
throw balls in the air,
give your parents a scare —
when you were young?

How about looking at stars,
planning trips up to Mars,
getting bruises and scars,
when you were young?

Did you wish to be older,
carry friends on your shoulders,
hate the nights that were colder —
Jesus, what was it like
when you were young?

TAKE A MOMENT . . .

What was your
favourite photograph
from the pilgrimage?

78

At the end of a long day pilgrims are hungry. Here are some of the foods you would eat while on a pilgrimage in Israel.

Religious Jews always take time to bless the food they eat. If you had a meal with a Jewish family, you might hear this blessing:

Blessed are you, Lord, God of all creation, for you feed the whole world with your goodness, with grace, with loving kindness and tender mercy. You give food to all creatures, and your loving kindness endures forever. Blessed are you, O Lord!

N E W   W O R D

pilgrimage:
a special journey to holy places.

Remember

With the child and his mother, Joseph went to the province of Galilee and made his home in a village called Nazareth.
(See Matthew 2: 21-23.)

Unit 5

When Jesus was twelve years old

A deep bow

One day a Japanese Buddhist was speaking to a group of people. They asked him, "How do you know there is a God? Does God exist?"

He answered with a story. "The other day," he said, "I was walking along the river. A gentle breeze was blowing. Suddenly the thought came to me — the air exists; I can feel it. I couldn't see it, but I knew that it was there because the wind was blowing against my face.

"And it was the same with the sun. Suddenly I became aware of its bright rays shining through the trees. I felt its warmth on my back. All this is completely free, I thought to myself — the gentle breeze, the bright, warm sun — they are simply there for us to enjoy.

"Without thinking about it at all, my two hands came together and I found myself making gassho — a deep bow. And then the thought came to me. That is all that matters — that we can bow, make a deep bow. Just that. Just that."

The Buddhist seems to be reverent here.
What is meant by "reverence?"

When we enter special, holy places, we often feel reverent. Read this story in the Bible about Moses' experience in a holy place.

One day, Moses was taking care of some sheep on the mountainside. Suddenly, he noticed fire coming from the middle of a bush. The bush was on fire, but it did not burn up! Moses said to himself, "I must go and look at this strange sight and see why the bush is not burned." As he came closer, he heard God call his name, "Moses, Moses." He answered, "Here I am." "Come no nearer," the Lord said. "Take off your shoes, for the place on which you stand is holy ground. I am the God of your father, the God of Abraham, the God of Jacob." (See Exodus 3: 1-6.)

Here are some special places. Why do you think they are sacred?

Do you have a sacred place?

How do you feel when you go there?

Jewish people have sacred places. The synagogue and the home are the two main places of prayer and worship.

For centuries, the Temple in Jerusalem was the most important "House of Prayer." Twice their enemies came and destroyed it.

When Jesus grew up the second temple was still being built. Today, all that is left of this second temple in Jerusalem is one wall, called the Western Wall. For Jews it is the holiest place on earth, and many go there to pray that their "wailing" for the loss of God's temple will change to songs of joy.

The Jewish people do not have their temple. "But," they say, "we will always be able to keep our faith as long as we have our home."

Western Wall — Jerusalem

Sharing a meal together is a sacred time for Jews. It is a time when special events are remembered and celebrated. That is why the family table is a holy place.

Another sacred place in some Jewish homes is a cupboard or tabernacle. Precious treasures are kept here:

- parchment or scrolls on which parts of the first five books of the Bible were written (Torah);

- the special embroidered clothes in which new-born babies were wrapped;

- the shrouds in which bodies of the dead were to be wrapped.

When Jesus first got up in the morning, he would say "Baruch Adonai" (ba' rook a'-do-ni) which means "Blessed be the Lord." He said other blessings when he washed and dressed and had his breakfast. But the most important morning prayer he learned is called the *Shema* (she-ma). "Shema" is the first word of the prayer. It means "Listen!"

"Listen, O Israel, The Lord our God is the one Lord. You shall love the Lord your God with all your heart, with all your soul, and with all your strength" (Deuteronomy 6: 4-5).

Jewish people repeat this prayer at noon and at night. Parents were to be sure to teach these words to their children. They even wrote them on parchment, put them in tiny boxes called a *phylactery* and wore them on their left arm and forehead. The words of the Shema are also kept in the mezuzah.

After Jesus rolled up his sleeping mat, he would watch Joseph tie his phylacteries on his left arm and forehead. Then Joseph would put on his prayer shawl or *tallith*. Joseph would then raise his arms in prayer.

Jewish people today often use these shawls during prayer. Women and girls do not have to pray at special times or wear a prayer shawl or skull cap (*yamelka*). But many want to do this. They say that putting on a tallith is like entering the "tent of God" to pray. It is like going into a holy place where one feels protected. "It is like resting in the palm of God's hand," they say.

On the doorway of every home is a *mezuzah* which means "doorpost." It is a small case and rolled up in it is a tiny piece of parchment with a verse from the Torah on it. People touch the mezuzah reverently as they go in and out and say this prayer: "The Lord God will guard my going and my coming, now and forevermore" (Psalm 121).

A holy day

The third commandment of the Lord is "Remember to keep holy the Sabbath day." Most Jewish people even today observe this law quite strictly. It is a day of rest and prayer. Sabbath means "rest." Jewish people of Jesus' time believed that even the animals should have a day off!

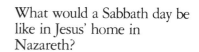

What would a Sabbath day be like in Jesus' home in Nazareth?

The Jewish *Sabbath* (Shabbat) begins at sunset on Friday and ends at sunset on Saturday. Friday therefore would be a very busy day for Mary because all the food had to be prepared beforehand. One could not even light a fire on this day of rest . . .

On Friday evening as the sun went down, the family welcomed the Sabbath. Mary would light the Sabbath candles. (It is always a woman or girl who does this in a Jewish family.) When the candles were lit, Mary would move her hands over them as though she were gathering up their warmth and light. She would then say a prayer of blessing something like this:

Come, let us welcome the Sabbath,
May its radiance light up our hearts
as we light these candles.

May the Lord bless us with
    Sabbath joy.
May the Lord bless us with
    Sabbath holiness.
May the Lord bless us with
    Sabbath peace.

After this, Joseph would raise a cup of wine and recite the *Kiddush* or Sabbath blessing. The cup was then passed around for all to share. After their first family meal on the Sabbath, everyone went to the synagogue.

On Saturday morning they went again. A special seven — branched candlestick called a *menorah* was lit and then the service began with the Shema: "Listen, O Israel . . ."

This picture tells a story.

Read Luke 2: 41-52 to see what it's all about.

TAKE A MOMENT. . .

Imagine you were in the Temple with Jesus. Is there something about Jesus that is special — something more than the way he answered questions?

Remember

"Why did you have to look for me? Did you not know I had to be in my Father's house?"
(See Luke 2: 49.)

Jesus goes about doing good

Juanita lay in bed in her new home in Charlottetown. She felt lonely. Everything was so different from Guatemala, where she had lived all her ten years — until today.

Mr. and Mrs. MacDonald had adopted her. Juanita liked them but felt strange with them. They did not speak Spanish and she knew no English. Juanita wondered what they were really like.

She tried to sleep, but tears kept her awake. Whenever she dozed off, she remembered her mountain home near Quetzaltenango — the golden corn that grew in little plots, the sheep who bleated on the side of the steep hills, and most of all her friends Maria and Gloria.

Then she remembered the sad things. The sound of gunfire, the funeral processions, people crying. If she could only get to sleep.

In the morning her new mother drove Juanita to school. Miss Kelly, her teacher, took her to the fourth-grade classroom and introduced her. The children clapped uncomfortably.

Juanita sat at the back. She felt alone and scared.

At noon Juanita waited until all the boys and girls had gone through the lunch line. She did not recognize any of the foods. She found an empty table and sat down by herself.

A few minutes later Amy came over and sat beside her. She smiled and pointed to Juanita's colourful, woven bracelet. Juanita pulled strands of coloured wool from her pocket and showed them to Amy.

Amy made some signs, asking Juanita if she really had made her own bracelet. Juanita smiled a big smile. Laying out the strands of wool, with Amy holding them against the table, she quickly braided a colourful bracelet. She tied the ends, made a loop and gave it to Amy.

Then something wonderful happened. Amy hugged her and took her to join some friends at their table.

Even though they couldn't speak Spanish, Juanita knew they were welcoming her. Everyone wanted one of her beautiful bracelets. And Juanita could feel their warmth.

Back in the classroom, Juanita felt alive again. She was still scared, but she belonged. She drew the bracelets she would make for her new friends, and a very special one for her new mother.

Life in Canada was looking better all the time.

(Adapted from *Her Friends Gave Juanita New Life*)

CHECK IT OUT . . .

What made Juanita feel alive again? How did she know she was being welcomed?

Do you know some persons like Amy? How do they make others feel?

Who cares?

To be caring persons we need to be noticing persons. We need to be persons who *see* and *hear* with our hearts!

When we look through our New Testaments we see many examples of Jesus showing us how to care. He sees the short little man, Zacchaeus, up in a big tree. He notices the disciples sending the children away. He hears Bartimaeus call out from the side of the road. For Jesus, the eyes and the ears are connected to the heart. And the signs of God's kingdom have to do with healing and forgiving, caring and loving.

See how many events you can find in your New Testament of Jesus showing us how to care.

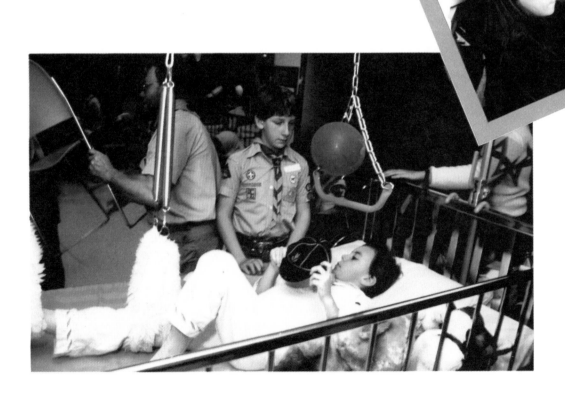

Remember Jesus' baptism. Jesus went down into the water and John baptized him in the Jordan. Do you remember what happened when Jesus came out of the water? Do you recall the words:

> "You are my Son, the Beloved; my favour rests on you" (Mark 1: 11).

Like the gentleness of a dove, God's Spirit filled Jesus' heart with peace and strength and love.

In this scene (in the synagogue in Nazareth) you can tell that Jesus is feeling strong with the power of God's Spirit. Listen to his words.

The spirit of the Lord has been given to me,
for he has anointed me.
He has sent me to bring the good news to the
*   poor,*
to proclaim liberty to captives
and to the blind new sight,
to set the downtrodden free,
to proclaim the Lord's year of favour.

                          Luke 4: 18-19

CHECK IT OUT...

One day Jesus' friends did not seem to understand something important Jesus had done. Find out what Jesus said to them in Mark 8: 17-21. Notice how strong Jesus' words are:

"Have you *eyes that do not see,
ears that do not hear?*"

When John the Baptist was in prison, he sent two messengers to Jesus asking him if he really is the one sent by God to save his people. Jesus answered:

"Go back and tell John what you have seen and heard: the blind see again, the lame walk, lepers are cleansed, the deaf hear, the dead are raised to life, and the Good News is proclaimed to the poor . . . ."

Read the message for yourself in Luke 7: 22.

Come and See

Refrain:

*Come and see —
What we've heard,
What we've seen,
What we've touched,
Jesus Christ
the Word of life*

1. *Jesus Lord, we have seen your kingdom
in many ways,
In loving hands, caring hearts
who do your will everyday
You have called us your friends
to build up your kingdom here,
By loving others, giving freely
and without fear.*

2. *Spirit come, give us strength to spread
the Lord's good news now,
May those who hear share our joy,
our peace and the Spirit's power.
Through our love, Lord, the deaf
will hear and the blind will see.
The lame will walk,
and all those in prison
will be set free.*

(© 1989 Timothy Crowley, CAPAC)

Remember

"... tell ... what you have seen and heard: the blind see again, the lame walk, lepers are cleansed, the deaf hear, the dead are raised to life, the Good News is proclaimed to the poor..." (Luke 7: 22).

"...sent to bring the good news...

At work!

What is going on in these pictures?
Have you ever visited a workplace?
Tell your story of the workers and
their work.

The work of hands and feet

This bulletin board is filled with scenes of
Jesus going about doing God's work —
touching, healing, celebrating, giving life.

Celebrating at Cana
John 2: 1-12

Curing the paralytic
Mark 2: 3-12

Curing
deaf m
Mark 7:

Curing the blind man
Luke 18: 35

Curing the leper
Luke 5: 12-14

Read about those events in the Gospels and answer these questions:

Whom did Jesus help?   Why did he help them?
How did he help them?   What did Jesus say?

Raising the
widow's son
Luke 7: 11-16

Curing a demoniac
Luke 4: 33-36

Healing a woman
on the Sabbath
Luke 13: 10-16

Preaching and
healing the sick
Matthew 4: 23-25

Cure of an
official's
son at Cana
in Galilee
John 4: 43-53

"Now Jesus was in one of the towns when a man appeared, covered with leprosy. Seeing Jesus he fell to the ground. 'Sir,' he said, 'if you want to, you can cure me.' Jesus stretched out his hand, touched him and said, 'Of course I want to! Be cured!'" (See Luke 5: 12-14.)

"And they brought him a deaf man who had an impediment in his speech; and they asked him to lay his hand on him" (Mark 7: 32).

"They came to Bethsaida, and some people brought to him a blind man whom they begged him to touch" (Mark 8: 22-26).

Have you ever wondered about the work of your hands?
Have you ever thought about how you use them?
What signs of the kingdom do you see on the bulletin board?
Make your own bulletin board.

Unit 6

They were all astounded and praised God

Excited family greets Joey in Metro

Homecoming a 'miraculous step' in long recovery, mom s

by Jack Lakey, *Toronto Star*

Joey Philion needed less than two hours to return to Canada, but the road to recovery will take years.

The courageous Orillia teenager — who has beaten overwhelming odds to survive third-degree burns to 95 per cent of his body — arrived at Metro's Hospital for Sick Children yesterday.

were met by excited famil members.

Dressed in a jaunty black fedora and Boston Red S sweatshirt, Joey was transferred to a Metro ambulance bus, taken by ferry to the foot of Bathurst St. and rushed to the 30-bed burn unit at Sick Kids.

A team of 11 burn specialists headed by plast surgeon Dr. Harold Clark began an immediate assessment of Joey's condition and started planning treatment.

'Felt good'

Linda Hawkins, Joey's mother, said the flight home symbolized a miraculous step in a battl that, at times, seemed insurmountable.

"I'm very surprised that i was so soon," Hawkins said of Joey's return. "We were thinking Christmas, at the earliest. Now we're hoping he'll be up to a da pass at Christmas."

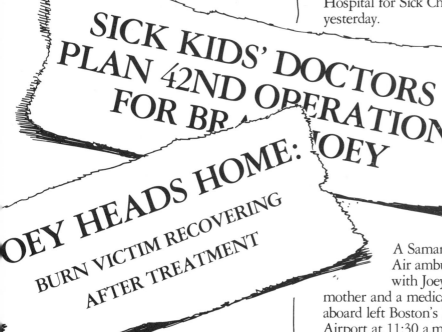

SICK KIDS' DOCTORS PLAN 42ND OPERATION FOR BR... JOEY

OEY HEADS HOME: BURN VICTIM RECOVERING AFTER TREATMENT

A Samaritan Air ambulance with Joey, his mother and a medical team aboard left Boston's Logan Airport at 11:30 a.m. and landed at Toronto Island Airport at 1:21 p.m. They

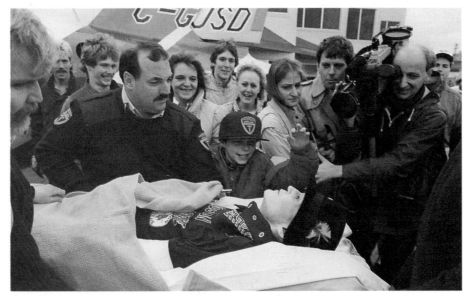

Joey Philion is greated at the Toronto Island Airport by his excited brother Danny.

Danny Hawkins, Joey's shy, 10-year old brother told reporters at a news conference he "felt really good" about having his big brother back.

When the two were reunited, "He said that he loved me and missed me and was just glad to see me," Danny said.

"Coming home makes him feel like he's made it. We're very close to being a family again," Joey's mom said.

"He wanted to live, that's why he's here," she said. "He fought with everything he had, and more."

For now, Joey wants to be close to his family and "do what normal 15-year-old boys do," Hawkins added. "Get back to school, his cadet group, and maybe learn to fly. We'll stick together."

(Reprinted with permission — The Toronto Star Syndicate)

How is the story astounding?
How is it a story of healing?

Do you know similar stories?
Look in your newspapers.

Giving praise and thanks

Go back to the bulletin board on pages 96 and 97. Do you remember the events? Read the stories again in your New Testament, this time watching for the people's reaction to Jesus. What did they say? How did they feel? What did they do?

Together with your friends, design several small flags and write the crowd's reaction. Use these questions to help you:

What is the name of the story? Where did it take place? What is the crowd's reaction?

". . . all the people were overjoyed at all the wonders he worked" (Luke 13: 17).

Thank you, God

Thank you, God,

for little things and big things,

for eyes to see with and ears to hear,

for new babies and for friends,

for hands and feet,

families and for fun.

Thank you God for . . .

Create a **litany** of praise and thanks and celebrate with your friends.

Remember

"A great prophet has appeared among us; God has visited his people" (Luke 7: 16).

Jesus is sent to bring God's love

Windy days

When the wind is in the south
The rain is in its mouth.

When the wind is in the east
It's good for neither man nor beast.

When the wind is in the north
The wise fisherman goes not forth.

When the wind is in the west
It sends us all the very best.

Have you heard this old weather
  rhyme?
What do you think it means?

Can we see the wind?
How do we know the wind is
  around us?

The parable of the Little River

In the heart of a great desert, Little River was searching its way through the burning sands to the Great Ocean. When the river had begun its journey, it was quick and bubbly and eager to travel. Now, as it twisted and turned among sharp rocks and hot sands, it had slowed down to a mere trickle.

One day, in the heat of the noonhour sun, it thought in its heart, "I can scarcely go on. I'm too thirsty, too hot, too weak. But I must struggle on, I must conquer these sands. I will win my way to the Great Ocean."

But as evening covered the desert in its dark shadows, the river was frightened and lonely. It was no longer sure that it was even headed in the right direction.

The Great Wind paused in its flight overhead. "Little River," she called. "Why do you struggle so, night and day?"

"To reach the Great Ocean." Then Little River added weakly, "Wherever it is."

The Great Wind laid her gentle hand upon the river's shoulders. "You can get there. You will. But you must trust me to help you. Do you want me to help you, Little River?"

The river paused. It had struggled so long the only way that it knew. The Great Wind understood its fears. "Yes," she assured the river. "You will have to change. But you can get to the Great Ocean if you are willing."

"Yes." The river had decided. "I am willing to change. Will you help me, Great Wind, that I may at last make my way to the Ocean?"

The Great Wind swept down immediately, taking the moisture from the river and drawing it up high into the air. High up into the night, away above the desert floor, river droplets were carried onward. Faster and faster, the wind soared on its way to the sea. Night faded and morning came, but on the river droplets flew, held securely in the arms of the Great Wind.

Late in the morning of the new day, a sparkle was seen in the distance. "Could it be?" wondered Little River. On they flew until below them the Great Ocean rolled and surged in welcome. And now the Wind drew back — she had done her part — and Little River swooped down into the shining depths of the waves. It plunged in among the great white squalls, cool and strong now after its desert trip. The Great Wind hovered, pleased that Little River had at last found its way.

The Great Ocean, the Great Wind, the happy little River — together they sparkled in the noonday sun.

THINK ABOUT IT . . .

What role did the Great Wind play?

What did the Little River decide to do? How was it difficult?

What did the Great Ocean do?

How is this a story of trust?

Nicodemus goes to Jesus

It was very dark that night. And through the streets of Jerusalem Nicodemus slipped quietly, making his way to the house where Jesus was staying. One of the disciples answered his knock and led him to Jesus. This was the moment Nicodemus had been waiting for; he had seen and heard wonderful things about this young Jewish rabbi. Here was Nicodemus, a man who seemed to have everything, and yet, he was uncertain. He felt moved in his heart to have a talk with Jesus so that somehow in the darkness of the night he might find light.

FINISH IT . . .

Open your New Testament to John 3: 1-18 and finish the story.

What kind of man do you think Nicodemus was?

How is the Little River like Nicodemus?

Jesus tells Nicodemus that he must *be born again of the Spirit*. What does Jesus mean?

What changes do you think Nicodemus might have to make?

Would these changes be easy to make?

THINK ABOUT IT . . .

". . . God loved the world so much
that he gave his only Son,
so that everyone who believes in him may not be lost
but may have eternal life" (John 3: 16).

The Holy Spirit leads us to God, into the ocean of God's love.

MAKE YOUR OWN . . .

Construct a weathervane out of cardboard and inscribe the words:

"The Spirit wind blows wherever it pleases."

Hang it in a place where it will catch the wind.

Remember

A Christian is one who has been born into a
new life *through water and the Spirit.*
(See John 3: 5.)

Unit 7

Jesus is the living water

Water, water everywhere

What makes water so special?

Make a list of all the ways we use it. What's your favourite way?

Water of life

It isn't funny, you know, that kind of thirst.

The kind of thirst I am talking about makes you feel like your whole body is sizzling. I know, because I felt that way when I was lost in the woods one hot summer day. I wandered for hours and hours, and I became very thirsty. Why wasn't there any water to drink, I kept asking myself. I felt like a plant that we had in the kitchen window at home, and which everyone forgot to water. It dried up so much that it crackled and fell apart.

That is how I felt, in fact — like I was going to crumble up and blow away in the wind.

We don't often think about it, but people can die with that sort of thirst. When there is so much water around, you do not really know what it is like. But when there is no water, when it becomes all that you can think about, then you know that it is a matter of life or death.

That day in the forest, I needed water so much that I started to faint. Fortunately, people were out looking for me, and eventually a couple of strangers were beside me, offering their water supply. They washed my face in it to cool me off. They spoke to me, and I knew that they wanted to help me. I was too weak to say anything more than "Thanks."

A bottle of water seems like a pretty everyday sort of thing. Except when you really need a drink. Then, holding that bottle is like holding the gift of life.

Without water, your life is going to be very, very short.

THINK ABOUT IT . . .

How would people who live in very dry areas feel about water?

How might these people help one another?

"Give me a drink."

". . . He came to the Samaritan town called Sychar, near the land that Jacob gave to his son Joseph. Jacob's well is there and Jesus, tired by the journey sat straight down by the well . . . . When a Samaritan woman came to draw water, Jesus said to her, 'Give me a drink'" (John 4: 5-7).

FINISH IT . . .

Open your New Testament to John's Gospel and hear the rest of the conversation.

What kind of water do you suppose Jesus was talking about when he said, ". . . anyone who drinks the water that I shall give will never be thirsty again"?

"*Come and see* a man who has told me everything I ever did; I wonder if he is the Christ?"

MAKE YOUR OWN . . .

Use clay to mold a table top scene of the event in the picture.

"Whoever drinks this water
will get thirsty again;
but anyone who drinks the water that I shall give
will never be thirsty again:
the water that I shall give
will turn into a spring inside him, welling up to eternal life."
John 4: 13-14

". . . anyone who drinks the water that
I shall give will never be thirsty again . . . ."
John 4: 14

Jesus shows us the Father

Have you ever heard someone say, "I couldn't see for looking"? What do you think this means?

No big deal

He passed by me everyday.

His hat, his coat — these were as familiar to me as the stop sign on the corner or the eight o'clock bus. Perhaps that is why, for months, I didn't even see him. He just passed by and kept on walking. I didn't notice him. I didn't even think about him. I just knew that he kept on walking.

I saw him on the street yesterday, and for the first time I thought, "I haven't seen him for a while." And, also for the first time, his wife was with him. They were walking together and talking and then, as if he knew what I was thinking, he looked my way and said, "Hello. Nice to see you." Then they both smiled, and you could see that they were very kind people, just out for a pleasant walk. Who is he, and where does he go each day?

It's no big deal, I admit. But tomorrow, when he passes by, I think I too will say, "Hello. Nice to see you."

Often, we are blind to the familiar things around us, the things that we think are "no big deal." But in our blindness, we miss many chances. What chance was almost missed in the story "No big deal"?

Can you suggest other chances or other truths we sometimes miss because we do not see what is around us?

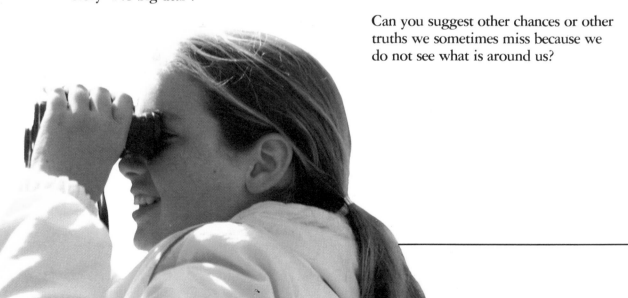

The Prince's great question

The Prince could no longer bear it. Everyday, he faced the same routine. His clothes were laid out for him, and someone said "Good morning, your majesty. You will wear the blue tunic this morning." A healthy breakfast was served to him to prepare him for the day's activities. "Good morning, your majesty. You will have oatmeal this morning." No one ever asked him what he wanted. It was so necessary that he be in good health that there was no choice at all. After all, what would happen to the kingdom if the Prince were to take sick, or even die?

"Your majesty, your lessons . . . Your majesty, archery practice awaits you . . . Your majesty, your presence is required in the drawing room." His majesty had had enough.

One morning, while he was practising his horsemanship, the Prince decided to take matters into his own hands. Galloping full tilt, he cleared the castle gates and headed for the distant forest. "At last," he thought to himself, "I have the freedom I have longed for. Now there is someone I must see, someone who will help me find meaning in this life I must lead."

On and on he rode, not quite sure of the direction he should take. Finally, he came to the bottom of a steep hill, and up near the top of the hill he could just barely make out the shape of a thatched hut. Tying his horse to the trunk of a nearby tree, he struggled up the slope until at last he reached his goal.

In a small patch of garden, a wise old woman bent over her carefully-tended bean plants. With great effort after his difficult climb, the young Prince straightened his shoulders and called to her, "Wise woman! I have come a great distance to talk to you. Please tell me, what is the meaning of this life I must lead?"

The woman continued at her work, carefully twining the stalks around a stake and fastening them to the support. The prince waited a few moments, and feeling that the wise woman was thinking over his great question, he sat down nearby to wait for her answer. After a while, when she still had not given him the answer he was looking for, he got up and took a stake from a pile lying on the ground. Without saying a word, he pushed the stake into the soil beside the bean plant next to the one the woman was working on. "Thank you," she said simply, and began tying up the next plant. The Prince placed another stake into the ground, and another, and another, until he and the woman had worked their way down the row of beans.

Having finished the work at hand, the Prince felt sure that the woman would reward him with an answer to his question. But at just that moment, a stranger appeared at the edge of the garden. "Help me!" he gasped, and collapsed upon the ground.

The Prince and the woman rushed to the stranger and carried him inside the hut. Finding a large wound on his leg, they set about cleaning and binding it. Then the Prince ran to get a dipper of water for the wounded man to drink, so that he would regain his strength. Finally, as evening approached, the stranger began to come round and was able to sit up and speak to them. Only then did the woman and the Prince realize how hungry they were, after all their work.

"I'll go and pick some of the fresh beans that we have tended," the Prince offered. And soon he returned to the hut with a basket of beans ready for cooking. In no time at all, the three of them were happily eating the beans and talking about the day's activity.

The Prince had almost forgotten his purpose in finding the wise woman. "Wise woman," he said to her, "You still have not told me the answer to my question. How will I find meaning in this life that I must lead?"

"You have already found the answer," the woman replied. "How is it that you do not see what that answer is?"

The Prince looked confused, so the woman helped him. "Today, when you came to see me, you helped me with my garden. Then, when this man came, you tended to his need with great care. If you hadn't, if he had to wait for attention, he might have died — you never know. And now, with your help, we have this meal to share together and to keep us going for another day. So the meaning in your life is clear: Help those around you. Help them now. In helping others, you have helped yourself." (Inspired by Leo Tolstoy.)

Seeing with new eyes

Jesus and his disciples had eaten well and, as they often did, they relaxed and talked after dinner. But Jesus' mood was different that night. He did not laugh and joke, but was serious, as he had been throughout the meal.

It was a holiday celebration, but the disciples too became serious and thoughtful. They had so many questions, so many puzzles that were not yet solved.

Philip said, "Lord, let us see the Father and then we shall be satisfied."

"Philip, we've been friends together all this time, and you still don't know me? To have seen me is to have seen the Father. Don't you believe that I am in the Father and the Father is in me? When I tell you about God the words are not from me; it is God the Father, living in me, who is speaking. You must trust me even if you don't understand. Look at my life and what I have been doing. Trust me for what I do; it is a sign that God is here."

(See John 14: 9-11.)

THINK ABOUT IT . . .

Do you think that Philip and the prince are a little alike?

What do we mean by "seeing with new eyes"? How about you?

The apostles were full of questions! Have you ever wondered what God is really like?

Have you ever asked questions like "Who made God?"

Write down some of your questions. Then, share your thoughts with your friends.

Remember

"If you know me, you know my Father too."
John 14: 7

Jesus goes up to Jerusalem

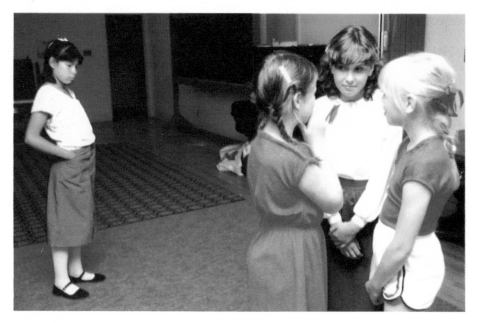

I went upstairs

I went upstairs to my room and I cried.
I cried because they just wouldn't understand
— because they wouldn't listen to me,
no matter how hard I tried
— because I was going to get punished,
and it wasn't even my fault.
God, why are they like this?
Why don't they try?
Why don't they hear?
I wonder, do they care?

THINK ABOUT IT . . .

Have you ever been blamed or
were you ever hurt when you
tried to be fair or kind?

"The Jewish Passover drew near, and many of the country people who had gone up to Jerusalem . . . looked out for Jesus, saying to one another as they stood about in the Temple, 'What do you think? Will he come to the festival or not?' The chief priests and Pharisees had by now given their orders: anyone who knew where he was must inform them so that they could arrest him" (John 11: 55-57).

Why did Jesus have enemies?

Jesus had gone about curing people and teaching and proclaiming the good news. It's hard for us to understand why some people wanted to arrest him.

Be the detective, and find out!

Here are two questions you need to prepare your case:

Did Jesus do anything wrong?

Why might people have been against him?

You can find clues in your New Testament by reading two or three of these passages:

Matthew 12: 9-14
Matthew 12: 22-24
Matthew 13: 53-58
Matthew 22: 15-22
Mark 2: 1-11

When you have put together your evidence, give your report.

Jesus decides

Jesus came back to Jerusalem, even though he knew that his enemies wanted to get rid of him. Perhaps he could have run away across the Jordan River to the desert. But he didn't.

Jesus went to Jerusalem because he knew he had to be faithful to his Father's message. In his heart there was a deep trust that his Father would not leave him to struggle alone.

Here comes the king!

— He's coming! He's coming!

— Where?

— Down the road, there, just past Old Isaac's fruit stand. Are you blind, that you can't see?

— Down there, where there's all that commotion? What's he riding on, anyway?

— A colt. It looks like David Ben Enan's. He keeps his animals in the pasture just beyond the east gate.

— Look at all those people! They're cutting branches from the trees and waving them at him. It looks as if they are servants, fanning him.

— Or as if they are soldiers, waving their spears.

Hosannah! Hosannah! Help us Lord! Hosannah!

— He's pretty important, isn't he! Strange, he doesn't look like he's rich or very special.

— He's important to some people, all right. But to others, well, that's a different story!

— They're out to get him, you mean?

— Exactly! The next few days will be a little edgy, I think.

— There's trouble coming then. That's too bad — Who do you say he is?

TAKE A MOMENT...

Read Mark's version of the story (Mark 11: 1-11).

A prayer of trust

Let us remember how Jesus was always faithful. He trusted in his Father's help. At the Last Supper, he reminded his friends to trust as well.

Leader: Sometimes we're weak and want to give up.
All: WE TRUST IN YOU, LORD.

Leader: Sometimes we are sad and we feel all alone.
All: WE TRUST IN YOU, LORD.

Leader: Sometimes we feel like being mean to each other.
All: WE TRUST IN YOU, LORD.

Leader: Sometimes we're afraid to stand up for what's right.
All: WE TRUST IN YOU, LORD.

Leader: Sometimes our friends turn against us and laugh.
All: WE TRUST IN YOU, LORD.

Leader: Sometimes we are blamed when we do something good.
All: WE TRUST IN YOU, LORD.

Continue on with the litany and end with the prayer . . .

Loving God, we thank you for your Son, Jesus, who has given us an example of trust and faithfulness. Amen.

"Do not let your hearts be troubled. Trust in God still, and trust in me."
John 14: 1

Unit 8

"... no greater love"

Whenever guests came to a Jewish house, a servant or slave would welcome them and wash their feet.

When Jesus was at the house of Simon the leper, he was not welcomed in the usual way. A woman came and washed his feet, and Jesus praised her for her love and care.

At the last supper, Jesus showed his love and care for his disciples when he did the job of a servant. They were amazed. They did not understand his actions.

Our tradition: our service

And Jesus said:
"Peter, won't you let me wash your feet as I have done for these others?"

— "Never! You will never wash my feet!"

"Why do you argue so? If I do not wash your feet, you can't have anything in common with me."

And Peter said:
"Jesus commanded me to look after his flock. I will wash the feet of the poor people of this city."

— "The poor, Peter! Do you really mean to get down on your knees in front of the poor?"

"Yes, of course. We are sent to care for each other, to serve everyone alike."

And Pope John Paul II said:
"Please permit me to wash your feet."

— "My feet?"

"Yes, Jesus tells us to care for each other as he cares for us. We are in this way part of what he was doing, many centuries ago."

And our Grade 4 teacher said:
"In this celebration, we recall how we must care for one another. We are all called to serve as Jesus did."

CHECK IT OUT . . .

Read in your New Testament the story of Jesus washing his disciples' feet, John 13: 12-15.

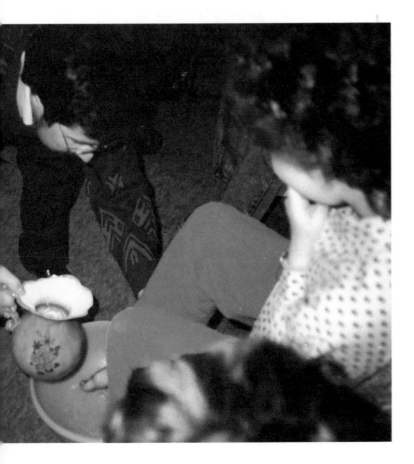

THINK ABOUT IT . . .

How would you feel if you were Peter and Jesus wanted to wash your feet?

How do you think Peter felt after the foot-washing?

Jesus has asked us to love and serve one another. What are some ways of doing this?

The eucharist is a "sacrifice of praise"

At the eucharist, we remember the last meal Jesus shared with his friends. Read the story in Matthew 26: 26-29.

We remember especially how Jesus gave himself for others:

> Blessed be Jesus, whom you sent
> to be the friend of children and
>   of the poor.
> He came to show us
> how we can love you, Father,
> by loving one another.
> He came to take away sin,
> which keeps us from being friends,
> and hate, which makes us
>   all unhappy.
> (From the Eucharistic Prayer for Children II)

Jesus' whole life was a sacrifice of praise. "Sacrifice" in this case means giving oneself to others.

We too ask God to help us be a living sacrifice of praise:

> Lord, look upon this sacrifice
>   which you have given to
>   your Church;
> and by your Holy Spirit,
>   gather all who share this
>   one bread and one cup
> into the one body of Christ,
>   a living sacrifice of praise.
> (From Eucharist Prayer IV)

Can you suggest some good ways for us to praise God in our lives?

Give yourself

When Old Mrs.
   Hennessey
Opened the door,
Susan saw parcels
And cards on the floor.
"It's my birthday,"
The old lady said
With a smile,
"I'm here all alone.
Can you stay for a while?"
And later while talking
She grew very sad:
"Now this is the eightieth
Birthday I've had.
Every year I get parcels
Piled up in the hall,
But rather than parcels
I'd love them to call.
I know you've worked hard
At your lessons all day.
I'm sure you'd prefer
To go out and to play.
I have beautiful cards
In a line on the shelf
But your present was
   nicest —
You gave me yourself.

Christy Kenneally

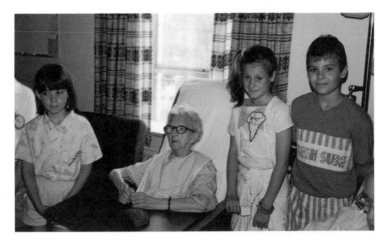

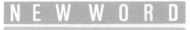

Eucharist:
thanksgiving.

THINK ABOUT IT . . .

In the poem, Mrs. Hennessey believes Susan gave herself as a present. How can you give yourself?

How might this giving be a "sacrifice of praise?"

Lord . . .
by your Holy Spirit,
gather all
who share
this one bread
and one cup
into . . . a living
sacrifice of
praise.
(From
Eucharistic
Prayer IV)

Jesus dies for us

Four questions

When they were at supper
and Judas decided to leave
Jesus watched him with eyes
that could scarcely believe —
After all of this time, Judas, why?

Out among the olive trees
When Jesus went off to pray
the disciples all slept —
scarcely heard Jesus say
"When I'm filled with such sorrow, friends, why?"

Next morning in the courthouse
there is a case to be won
but Pilate can't see:
"What harm has he done?
You all want him crucified — why?"

In darkness, about the ninth hour
Jesus looks at the faces around.
He sees eyes that are filled with hatred
and soldiers all holding their ground.
He hears noise and confusion and laughter
and knows that it's his turn to die.
In his last and loneliest moment,
he cries, "Oh, my God! Father — why?"

How do you think Jesus felt as Judas left?

Remembering the work you did as a detective, why do you think people wanted Jesus crucified?

What feelings do you think Jesus had when he asked "Why" (last line)?

Following the way of Jesus

During Holy Week in Jerusalem, the early Christians used to follow the route taken by Jesus as he carried his cross to Calvary. Along the way, they would pause for prayer and remember what happened to Jesus. The places where they stopped were known as "stations," and over the years the number came to be fixed at fourteen. The tradition grew of having pictures of the stations in churches around the world, so that Christians could follow the way of the cross in their own parishes.

Have you noticed the stations of the cross in your parish? Take the time to see them during the next few weeks. Meanwhile, take a moment and turn the page to see some of the stations.

The first station:

Jesus is condemned to death

Father, where is the justice in this? I was with them every day, but today they treat me like a criminal. I will not answer their charges. But I can't shut out their faces.

The fourth station:

Jesus meets his mother

Here is my mother, who protected me from harm. Today, she is helpless. There is nothing she can do. — There is nothing I can do for her.

The fifth station:

Simon of Cyrene helps Jesus to carry the cross

Father, what a strange twist this is! Here is someone doing me a favour, helping me to carry my burden. And speeding me toward my death. What a day is this, when everything is turned upside down. The good things I have done now seem bad in their eyes.

The eighth station:

Jesus speaks to the women

Father, as I struggle with my painful steps, here are women who are struggling too. Struggling with their feelings. How can I help them? Their tears should be for themselves. There are many different types of suffering.

The twelfth station:

Jesus dies on the cross

"My God, my God, why have you abandoned me?"

The fourteen stations of the cross.

The fourteenth station:

Jesus is laid in the tomb

"When it was evening, there came a rich man of Arimathaea, called Joseph, who had himself become a disciple of Jesus. This man went to Pilate and asked for the body of Jesus. Pilate thereupon ordered it to be handed over. So Joseph took the body, wrapped it in a clean shroud and put it in his own new tomb which he had hewn out of the rock. He then rolled a large stone across the entrance of the tomb and went away. Now Mary of Magdala and the other Mary were there, sitting opposite the sepulcher." Matthew 27: 57-61

Unit 9

He who was crucified is risen

Христос Воскрес! Воістину Воскрес!
CHRIST IS RISEN! HE IS RISEN INDEED!

Easter lilies everywhere! The church looked like, and smelled like, a flower garden. Somehow, the lights seemed brighter than they usually did and the posters which had been put up for Easter picked up the glow. Everything seemed alive.

Most lively of all, however, was Father Don himself. He told us of an eastern European custom of people greeting each other on Easter Sunday. "He is risen!" Father would yell at us. And we were all to yell back, "Truly he is risen!"

And so it went. Throughout the Mass, just when you thought he might have forgotten it, Father would pause, grin at all of us, and yell "He is risen!" He said it with such energy that it seemed like he was really surprised — that the news was too good to be true.

"Truly he is risen!" We kept saying it over and over again, as if we were the disciples and we had just found out.

Have you ever had such good news that you just couldn't believe it? What do you think you would do? What do you suppose the disciples did when they heard, for the first time, *the good news?*

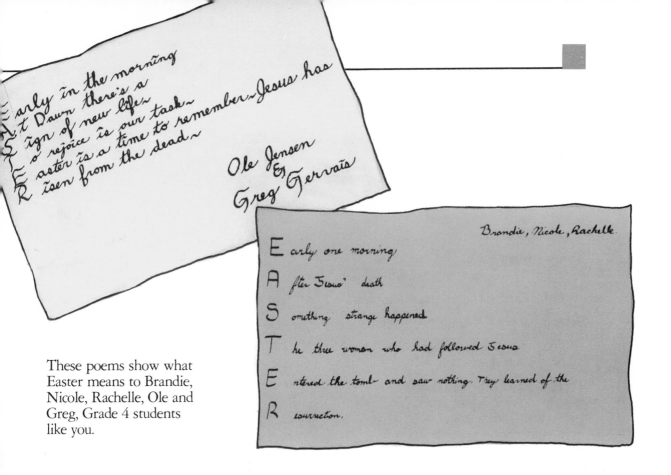

Early in the morning
At Dawn there's a
sign of new life~
To rejoice is our task~
Easter is a time to remember~Jesus has
risen from the dead~

Ole Jensen
&
Greg Gervais

Brandie, Nicole, Rachelle

E arly one morning

A fter Jesus' death

S omething strange happened

T he three women who had followed Jesus

E ntered the tomb and saw nothing. They learned of the

R esurrection.

These poems show what Easter means to Brandie, Nicole, Rachelle, Ole and Greg, Grade 4 students like you.

What does Easter mean to you?

Jesus loved a picnic

How is the fishing out there?

— Terrible.   It would have to improve to be just bad!

Have you caught any fish?

— Not a single one.   And we've worked all night!

Throw the net out to starboard. Have you found something now?

— Fish! Fish!   There's more than we can handle out here!

Peter, what are you doing?

— I'm going ashore.   This boat is too slow!

There is bread here, and the fish are cooking. Come, friends. I am with you once more. We have every reason to celebrate. Won't you come and eat the breakfast I have made for you? You know how I've always loved a picnic!

THINK ABOUT IT . . .

How do you think the disciples are feeling at first? Why?

How do you think they would feel when they recognize Jesus on the shore?

Jesus has bread and fish ready for the disciples to eat. In what other stories do you remember Jesus feeding people?

Plan for a picnic

Bread (to be broken and shared with everyone)
Fish (enough to nourish and give strength)
Forgiveness (a large amount — some will need two or three helpings, especially Peter)
Reassurance (plenty for everyone)
Love (enough to last them forever)
Kindling and matches (to build the campfire, to help guide them to shore, to cook and give warmth and comfort to all)
Pack and bring at dawn to the Sea of Tiberias

CHECK IT OUT . . .

Read for yourself the story of the breakfast on the seashore, John 21: 1-17.

Easter is the
greatest feast
of the Church
year because it
is the celebration
of Jesus'
resurrection from
the dead.

"We have seen the Lord"

Who do you say God is?

Some say money,
Some say wealth,
Some say happiness,
Some say youth.
Many say ideas,
like freedom
and insight
and science . . .
But you,
who do you say
God is?

CHECK IT OUT . . .

Do you remember what Peter said about Jesus, and who he is?

Read Matthew 16: 13-20 in your New Testament.

True knowledge of who Jesus is did not come easily. God revealed the truth about Jesus to Peter, but still Peter tended to forget when he was in danger. We saw this on Good Friday. Here is another story about a disciple who had a hard time believing the truth about who Jesus is.

In the evening, the disciples gathered in a room they all knew well. Together, they were a little happier, a little more protected from the dangers they all felt around them. So many things had happened — some terrible things. And now there was this other news. No one knew what would happen next.

Suddenly, Jesus was there, standing among them. "Peace be with you," he said. And they all drew back as if they didn't know him. He showed them the marks in his hands and again said "Peace be with you." He talked to them, and they knew it was really Jesus.

But where was Thomas? He was not with them as they huddled together in the room. When he arrived, they all rushed to tell him, "We have seen the Lord."

Thomas was a man who was not easily persuaded. "Unless I see the marks on his hands and feet, I won't believe what you are saying."

Several days later, when the whole group was together again, Jesus once more came and stood among them. He looked steadily at Thomas: "Put your finger into the holes in my hands. Give me your hand — put it here, into my side. Doubt no longer, but believe."

Thomas was overcome. "My Lord and my God!"

(See John 20: 19-28.)

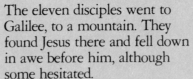

The eleven disciples went to Galilee, to a mountain. They found Jesus there and fell down in awe before him, although some hesitated.

(See Matthew 28: 16-17.)

Remember

Christians call Jesus "Lord" because God raised him from the dead and gave the whole world into his care.

Unit 9

"Now at last they know"

What colour's a hug?

I remember once when I watched a show I wasn't supposed to. We aren't really allowed to watch scary things, but this time I got away with it.

The show was really creepy. There was this house, and it kept doing things to the people who lived in it. They never knew when something bad was going to happen. Even though I knew while I was watching that it was really just pretend, I still wondered "What if?"

I couldn't sit still for the whole thing. When my mom came in, I was buried under the pillows on the couch, with the TV still on because I was too scared to get up and turn it off. She didn't yell or anything. I guess she figured I'd learned my lesson. She just took the pillows away and hugged me close.

My mom is nicer than a haunted house.

THINK ABOUT IT . . .

Can you think of times when you needed to have someone hold you and protect you?

IMAGINE FOR A MOMENT . . .

What colour is your favourite hug?

There are many stories in the Bible of people who have become open to God. These people discover that God is always with them, protecting and comforting them. Turn the page and read the prayer psalm that expresses the feelings that go with this discovery.

Psalm 138

Before I was born,
you made each little part of me in secret.

While I was hidden in my mother's womb,
you watched me grow.
You saw my bones begin to form
and join together.

From the first moment of my life
you knew me!

I praise you, Lord,
and I am filled with wonder.
For everything you do
is strange and marvellous.

*God the Father is never far away
— he loves us too much
to leave us all on our own.
That's why we praise him!*

You know me, Lord, so very well,
you know when I get up.
You know when I go back to sleep,
you know each thing I do.

You know what I am going to say
before I even speak!
You are *always* close to me.
You're wonderful, O Lord.

So if I climb the highest hill,
you would be there with me.
And if I swam beneath the waves,
you'd still be there with me.

Even in the dark at night
you would be next to me.
Yes, even then I could not hide,
you would be there with me.

(From *Praise* by A.J. McCallen)

***I am hiding in
the popcorn.***
(Liam Durnin)

***I am hiding between
the pillows of the couch.***
(Angie MacNeil)

WRITE IT DOWN . . .

Finish the sentence in your remembering book. "Even if I hid _____ you would still be there." Draw a picture of yourself in your hiding place. Do you feel God's presence there?

*I would hide
in an apple tree.*
(Rita Khouri)

Jesus too had a special prayer to comfort his disciples before he died. He wanted them to feel protected and strengthened, because he would not be with them for much longer. This is how he prayed:

*Father, the hour has come:
I have finished the work
that you gave me to do.
I have made your name known
to these you have given to me.
Now at last they know
that all you gave me comes
indeed from you;
for I have given them
the teaching you gave to me.
I pray for them
because they belong to you.
Protect them
and consecrate them in the truth.
May they all be one
as we are one.
May the love with which you
love me be in them,
so I may be with them.*
(See John 17: 1-26.)

Jesus' story is our story

The rainbow day (September 18, 1984)

Everybody in Fort Simpson was excited. For months they had been preparing for the Pope's visit, and now everything was ready. The special tent, the buckskin vestments, the warm welcome for Pope John Paul. Many of the children were so excited that they could scarcely contain themselves. "He'll soon be here!"

It was dark when the Pope left Edmonton. But as his plane drew closer to Fort Simpson, a heavy fog rolled in and smothered the entire area. Impossible to land in such a fog! The plane circled high above Fort Simpson as those on the ground gazed upward. They could hear the plane, but they recognized that their welcome would have to wait.

No miracle occurred. The fog did not lift. Disappointed, Pope John Paul had to return to Vancouver. Everyone in Fort Simpson was left to put away the memories of a visit that didn't happen.

But the Pope did not leave without giving something to the people left waiting for him. He spoke to them over the radio, promising that with God's help he would return and have his visit with them after all.

(September 20, 1987)

Three long years passed before another opportunity came up. Then, John Paul's plane at last touched down in Fort Simpson. The morning had been a wet one, with grey clouds and plenty of rain. But as the Pope walked among the hundreds of people gathered to welcome him, the sun burst out and a magnificent rainbow bridged the sky.

The promise was kept.

Promises, promises

I've made promises
that I can't keep —
like I'll keep my room clean
for the rest of my life,
like I'll never ever
hit my brother again,
like get me out of this one, God,
and I'll never tell another lie.
But a promise was made to me,
a promise I know won't be broken:
"I'll love you in daylight or dark
as I did before you were born."

Luke tells us about a promise that Jesus made to his followers before he returned to his Father. For forty days, he had been showing himself alive, and his friends were filled with joy. Now, as he was ready to leave them, he told them to stay in Jerusalem for what the Father had promised. That promise was the help his followers needed to continue his work: "You will receive power when the Holy Spirit comes on you, and then you will be my witnesses not only in Jerusalem but throughout Judaea and Samaria, and indeed to the ends of the earth."
(Acts 1: 8)

**THINK
ABOUT IT . . .**

What would this power from the Holy Spirit do for the disciples?

What did Jesus mean by being a "witness?"

Helped by the Holy Spirit on Pentecost, the disciples lost their fear and dared to speak openly about the truth Jesus had taught them. Here is a story about Peter, and how he spoke to the people of Jerusalem for the first time:

Peter, the fisherman. Peter, the terrified man who denied that he even knew Jesus. This same Peter now stood before the learned and holy men of Jerusalem and shouted: "All you who live in Jerusalem, make no mistake about this. Listen carefully to what I have to say!"

And he told them about Jesus, how he had lived and died, and how God had raised him from the dead. Peter also told his listeners about the gifts of the Holy Spirit, which Jesus had promised.

"You must be baptized in the name of Jesus Christ and receive the gift of the Holy Spirit. This promise was made for you and for your children."

Many people heard what Peter was saying and were baptized. The word of Jesus was beginning to spread.

Remember

". . . You will receive power when the Holy Spirit comes on you, and then you will be my witnesses . . ." (Acts 1: 8).

Unit 10

Jesus' mission is our mission

Discipling

I'd like to show before I go
what it's all about
so I'm going to shout —

"This is where I've been!
Do you know what I've seen?"
Going to spread the word,
Tell them all I've heard —

I just can't sit still
with this news!

A disciple is anyone who comes to know Jesus and follows him. By "following" we mean living in a way that is patterned after Jesus' life. We have seen how Jesus helped people, how he taught them and did the will of his Father.

THINK ABOUT IT . . .

Who are the people you have met in this year's program whom you would call disciples?

How did these memory people help you to know God better?

Thank you, Peter, for coming our way,
you showed us that our doubts, like yours, can all
be swept away.

Thank you, Nicodemus, for coming our way,
you showed us that by braving the night we still
might find the day.

Thank you, Nonna, for coming our way,
you helped us bake the Easter bread and taught
what traditions say.

Thank you, Joey Philion, for coming our way,
you taught us that even when we hurt, we still can
hope and pray.

Thank you, Jesus, for being with us every day,
you teach us how to care for those we meet along
the way.

FINISH IT . . .

Add your favourite
memory persons to the
list, showing
how they helped you to
know God better.

My memory person is Mrs. Baglole,
She takes time to prepare and teach our
lessons, she was a volunteering teacher
to teach a class that most people
thought would be hard to teach,
1. She is our catechist,
2. Took time to teach us,
3. She taught us all about Jesus,

Chris

Do you remember the secret code you drew or painted onto your pendant at the beginning of the year? Your code told a story about you — who you are and what things you treasure.

The early Christians also had a code like yours. It was kept secret because they had many enemies who wanted to stamp out the new religion that was spreading so quickly. That secret code is known as the Apostles' Creed.

The Apostles' Creed

I believe in God, the Father almighty,
creator of heaven and earth.
I believe in Jesus Christ, his only Son, our Lord.
He was conceived by the power of the Holy Spirit
and born of the Virgin Mary.
He suffered under Pontius Pilate,
was crucified, died, and was buried.
He descended to the dead.
On the third day he rose again.
He ascended into heaven,
and is seated at the right hand of the Father.
He will come again to judge the living and the dead.

I believe in the Holy Spirit,
the Holy catholic Church,
the communion of saints,
the forgiveness of sins,
the resurrection of the body,
and the life everlasting.

Living as Jesus' disciples

By sharing our time....

By including everyone...

By forgiving those who have hurt us...

By sharing a meal, especially with those who are less fortunate...

istening to others...

By visiting the
sick or disabled...

Unit 10

We celebrate our story

Come and see

Chorus:
Come and see!

Student #1:
What do you want me to see?

Chorus:
Come and see what happens when seeds are sown in your garden plot.

Mime:
(One student broadcasts seeds, while three others tumble down, all curled up as seeds. Another pretends to water the garden and the seeds start to uncurl. One grows straight and tall, one grows part way and then bends over, the other does not grow at all but stays almost fully curled up.)

Student #1:
One seed has grown into a healthy tall plant. What happens to it now?

Chorus:
Come and see!

Mime:
(All but the straight plant resume their places in the semicircle. Another student comes and "picks" the plant by causing it to fall back down to the ground, then goes through the motions of kneading bread with the fallen seed as part of the dough. The student who has played the part of the plant then resumes her or his place in the semicircle, leaving the baker-student to go through the rest of the motions of making bread.)

Student #2:
The seed is now part of a larger loaf. It had to fall and die to become part of this recipe. But what's the use of this loaf of bread?

Chorus:
Come and see!

Student #3:
What do you want me to see?

Chorus:
See how this loaf of bread becomes a breakfast
on the shore.

Mime:
(The student who has made the bread pretends to
cook over a campfire, then three other students
come up, hauling imaginary fishing nets as they
walk. The student over the fire offers some of the
bread to each of the other students, then places a
hand on the shoulder of one.)

Chorus:
Come and see!

Student #4:
What do you want me to see?

Chorus:
Come and see how these disciples are sent into gardens all over the world.

Mime:
(The baker-student leaves the others, spreading hands out indicating that the others should go out in all directions. Each disciple-student goes out to the semicircle, whispers to someone else and then leads that person into the centre.)

Student #5:
What is the message that these people give?

Chorus:
Come and see!

Acknowledgements

Come and See, Year 4 Student Text, is a catechetical resource of the "Born of the Spirit" series, written and produced by the National Office of Religious Education, Canadian Conference of Catholic Bishops, Ottawa, Canada.

Approved by:
Most Rev. Adam Exner, Most Rev. Marcel A. J. Gervais, Most Rev. Frederick B. Henry, Most Rev. Joseph Faber MacDonald, Canadian Conference of Catholic Bishops.

Coordinating Editor:
Muriel Loftus

Production Manager:
Joyce Harpell

Contributors:
Donna Kerrigan, Myrtle Power, pilot teams and students from across Canada

Word Processing:
Simonne Carr

Excerpts from THE JERUSALEM BIBLE, copyright © 1966 by Darton, Longman & Todd, Ltd. and Doubleday, a division of Bantam, Doubleday, Dell Publishing Group, Inc. Reprinted by permission.

Excerpts from the English translation of *The Roman Missal* © 1973, International Committee on English in the Liturgy, Inc. (ICEL); excerpts from the English translation of *Eucharistic Prayers for Masses with Children* © 1975, 1980, ICEL. All rights reserved. Used with permission.

English translation of the Apostles' Creed by the International Consultation on English Texts.

Excerpts adapted from GRANDMA'S BREAD produced by Franciscan Communications, 1229 S. Santee St., Los Angeles, CA 90015; Canadian Distributor — Claude Primeau & Associates LTD., 1035 North Service Rd., Oakville, Ontario L6H 1A6. Used with permission.

JESUS WAS THE STORYTELLIN' KIND from EXPERIENCING JESUS by Mark Link. © Copyright 1984 by Tabor Publishing, 25115 Avenue Stanford, Valencia, CA 91355. Used with permission.

Stories GIFT OF JOY and HER FRIENDS GAVE JUANITA NEW LIFE by Janaan Manternach. Copyrighted by the NC News Service. Reprinted with permission.

Excerpts from MOTHER THERESA by Mary Craig. Reprinted with permission of the publisher Hamish Hamilton Ltd., 27 Wrights Lane, London W8 5TZ.

Excerpts from the BASQUE SHEEPHERDER AND THE SHEPHERD'S PSALM by James K. Wallace. Reprinted with permission of the National Wool Growers Association, NATIONAL WOOL GROWER magazine.

Poem I AM THE LIGHT, adapted. Copyright © 1986, Donna Kerrigan. Used with permission.

EXCITED FAMILY GREETS JOEY IN METRO by Jack Lakey (TSS). Reprinted with permission — The Toronto Star Syndicate.

Illustrations by:
Eugene Kral

Photographs by:
Location of photographs on a given page is indicated by:
L — left, C — centre, R — right, T — top, B — bottom, or combinations,
such as BLC — bottom left centre,
and BL/C — bottom left and centre.

Micha Bar AM, Magnum: 72R, 84T, 86B
Gilbert Beers: 72L, 74L/T, 75T, 77
Berkeley Studio, United Church of Canada: 17CR, 60, 62T, 81TL/TR, 90BC, 94B, 120, 126, 137C
Gilles Boily: 47C
Skip Brooks: 99R
By permission of the British Library: 24
Bernie Caroll: 12CR, 95B, 151L
Terry Cherwick: 12C
Dorothy Chocolate, Native Press: 148
Adrienne Corti: 59
Courtesy of Franciscan Communications, Gavin Griffith, OFM: 128-129
Courtesy of Niagara Falls Art Gallery — "Passion of Christ" by Wm. Kurelek: 143
Courtesy of Pacific Rim National Park, Barry Campbell: 36
Courtesy of Pilot Teachers: 10, 14, 15, 17T, 19, 79, 125, 127
Courtesy of Secretary State: 12TR, 62C, 81B
Courtesy of Terence Lozynsky: 65
Jack Dowling: 91TC, 138-139, 147
P. Flemington, Berkeley Studio: 55TC
Leonard Freed, Magnum: 84B
Paul Fusco, Magnum: 76, 82T
Jean Guy Goulet: 6LR
Joyce Harpell: 44L, 47T, 48, 80, 91C, 92BR, 95R, 103T
Israel Museum: 13
Wolf Kutnahorsky, Berkeley Studio: 55R/B, 98BL/BR
W. McLennan, Museum of Anthropology, UBC: 37
Benoit Mainville: 78C
Peter Marlow, Magnum: 86T

Fred Miller: 54L
Janine Murdoch: 31
National Gallery of Canada, Ottawa — "Presentation in the Temple" by John Opie: 69
Ottawa Citizen: 95T
Mike Pinder: 12BR, 32C/TR/CR, 110-111
Marilyn Silverstone, Magnum: 83
Lu Taskey: 18BL, 151R
Emil Telizyn: 17BL, 26, 44R, 63, 136
Toronto Star Synidcate: 101
Ron Tourangeau: 58, 73, 82
Vince Van Zutphen: 71, 74R, 75B
Bill Wittman: COVER, 6, 12BL, 17CL/BR, 18TR, 21, 32BR, 43, 45, 54R, 57, 62BL, 66, 67, 78T/B, 81C, 85, 91B, 94TR, 98C, 103 except T, 115, 116, 130-135, 137L/R, 140, 145, 149, 151C
Pilot Student Artwork: 20, 104-105, 137, 140, 146, 153, 155-157

Design by:
Banfield-Seguin Ltd., Ottawa

Colour separations by:
Hadwen Graphics Ltd., Ottawa

Printed and bound in Canada by:
John Deyell Company

Published by:
Publications Service, Canadian Conference of Catholic Bishops, 90 Parent Avenue, Ottawa, ON Canada K1N 7B1

ISBN 0-88997-197-8

Legal deposit: National Library, Ottawa, ON Canada.